NAZI IDEOLOGY

and the HOLOCAUST

UNITED STATES HOLOCAUST MEMORIAL MUSEUM

LIBRARY OF CONGRESS
CATALOGING-IN-PUBLICATION DATA

Nazi ideology and the Holocaust.
p. cm.
Includes bibliographical references and index.
ISBN-13: 978-0-89604-712-9
ISBN-10: 0-89604-712-1
1. World War, 1939-1945—Atrocities.
2. Genocide—Germany—History—20th century.
3. National socialism. I. United States Holocaust
Memorial Museum.
D804.3.N43 2007
940.53'18—dc22

2007038045

CONTENTS

Maps:

This publication is made possible by a generous grant
from the Hess, Ein, and Lewin Families in loving memory
of Charles and Ilse Hess.

RESEARCH, WRITING, AND EDITING

William F. Meinecke Jr., *Historian*

Alexandra Zapruder, *Consultant*

Timothy Kaiser, *Project Director*

Laura Glassman and Barbara Hart
of Publications Professionals, *Copy Editors*

REVIEW

Peter Black, *Senior Historian*

Sarah Ogilvie, *Director of the National Institute
for Holocaust Education*

Steven Luckert, *Permanent Exhibition Curator*

Susan Bachrach, *Special Exhibitions Curator*

Edward Phillips, *Deputy Director of Exhibitions*

Daniel Napolitano, *Director of Education*

DESIGN AND PRODUCTION

Studio A, Alexandria, Va.

UNITED STATES HOLOCAUST MEMORIAL MUSEUM

Fred Zeidman, *Chairman*

Joel M. Geiderman, *Vice Chairman*

Sara J. Bloomfield, *Director*

The Museum also acknowledges the contribution of
the following individuals to the production of this book:

Victoria Barnett	Andrea Lewis
Lea Caruso	Wendy Ng
Amy Donovan	Bruce Tapper
Stephen Feinberg	

BETWEEN 1933 AND 1945, GERMANY'S GOVERNMENT, LED BY ADOLF HITLER AND THE National Socialist (Nazi) party, carried out a deliberate, calculated attack on European Jewry. Basing their actions on antisemitic ideology and using World War II as a primary means to achieve their goals, they targeted Jews as their main enemy, killing six million Jewish men, women, and children by the time the war ended in 1945. This act of genocide is now known as the Holocaust. As part of their wide-reaching efforts to remove from German territory all those whom they considered racially, biologically, or socially unfit, the Nazis terrorized many other groups as well, including Roma (also known as Gypsies), Germans with mental and physical disabilities, homosexuals, Jehovah's Witnesses, Poles, and Soviet prisoners of war. In the course of this state-sponsored tyranny, the Nazis left countless lives shattered and millions dead.

Much has been written about what took place during the era of the Holocaust and where, when, and how the Nazis carried out their murderous plans. To fully comprehend the Nazis' actions, however, one must consider and understand the theoretical underpinnings that led them to conceive of such plans in the first place. In other words, what did the Nazis believe and how did they put their theories into practice?

Adolf Hitler formulated and articulated the ideas that came to be known as Nazi ideology. Born in a small town in Austria, Hitler had failed as an art student before becoming a corporal in the German army. Like many of his countrymen, he was embittered and humiliated by Germany's defeat in World War I and was further outraged by the terms of the Versailles Treaty, which had been signed in 1918 and which required the vanquished nation to give up vast territories and to pay heavy war debts.

Hitler joined the nascent Nazi party in the early 1920s, finding a political home among others who despised Germany's democratic Weimar government—established immediately following Germany's defeat in World War I—and who blamed Marxists and Jews for the country's problems. Hitler used his personal charisma to rise to the top of the radical, militant party, soon becoming its leader. Amid economic crisis and social unrest throughout Germany, the ranks of the Nazis swelled to 50,000 by 1923.

That same year, Hitler and the Nazi party attempted a coup, called the Beer-Hall Putsch, but failed to seize control of the government. In the trial that followed, Hitler was sentenced to five years in prison for treason. There, he wrote his political autobiography, *Mein Kampf (My Struggle)*, in which he outlined his vision of a new future for Germany. In his book, Hitler stated that he first became an active antisemite during his formative years in Vienna, where he became familiar with social Darwinism. That theory sought to apply Charles Darwin's theory of natural selection to human society, imagining all of human history as a struggle for primacy between social groups, whether defined by race, ethnicity, nation, or class. He also incorporated in his writing elements of Malthusian economics, a theory suggesting that the earth's finite ability to produce food, as well as its cycles of disease and natural disaster, inherently limited population growth. Finally, Hitler combined those theories with writing about the nationalist German notion of "blood and soil" (*Blut und Boden*), which glorified peasant life and idealized the land. From this composite of social, economic, historical, and mystical elements, Hitler adapted and skillfully propagated an ideology that put the necessity of racial struggle at the center of human affairs.

Hitler was convinced that he had found the key to comprehending an extraordinarily complex world. He believed that a person's characteristics, attitudes, abilities, and behavior were determined by his or her so-called racial makeup. In Hitler's view, all groups, races, or peoples (he used those terms interchangeably) carried within them traits that were immutably transmitted from one generation to the next. For better or for worse, no individual could overcome the innate qualities of race.

Although most people accept the notion of an *individual* human impulse to survive, Hitler, like other social Darwinists, believed that all members of a race or ethnic group shared a *collective* instinct for survival. In his view, the continuation of a race primarily depended on the ability of its members to pass on its innate characteristics to succeeding generations. This notion translated to an abhorrence of intermingling between peoples, because it would lead to the pollution of the distinguishing elements of the race and, in turn, to the degeneration of its very nature. According to this thinking, this process could, over time, threaten and potentially extinguish an entire race.

The second element in Hitler's theory of survival involved the need to acquire "living space" (*Lebensraum*). Each race, he asserted, was driven to struggle with others for room in which to grow and for resources on which to thrive. "Every being strives for expansion," he said in a speech in Erlangen, Germany, in November 1930, "and every nation strives for world domination." Those who were successful in this territorial competition would continue to expand their numbers, thereby overwhelming the smaller populations around them. The lesser races, weakened by a lack of living space, would eventually stagnate and die out. In the end, he judged the success or failure of each race by the size of its population and the area of territory it controlled: a great nation occupied a huge area of land; a weak one held little or none. The road map to racial survival depended not on peaceful coexistence with one's neighbors but on defeating them in the quest for limited resources.

In Hitler's mind, however, the struggle for survival was not a neutral contest in which all races were different but equally entitled to supremacy. Instead, he believed in a hierarchy of racial groups in which some were inherently gifted—possessed of traits such as integrity, intelligence, and beauty—whereas others were fundamentally flawed by nature and were devious, stupid, or ugly. Because he held that all racial groups shared the same drive for collective survival (competing against one another for finite resources and space in which to grow), and because he thought that racial mixing diluted good characteristics and spread bad ones, Hitler viewed those races at the top of the hierarchy as being at risk of infiltration and destruction by those at the bottom. To survive, a superior race must not only separate itself from lesser ones but also continue to suppress and dominate those who would threaten to overtake it.

Hitler imagined himself as a savior, applying his theoretical construct of racial struggle to the specific case of Germany. He condemned the democratic Weimar Republic as weak and ineffectual. Moreover, he felt the country's leaders had led the nation dangerously astray and had corrupted the German soul by overemphasizing the intrinsic worth of the individual. To Hitler, individuality was an egoistic and culture-corroding value because it duped people into forgetting about and thereby relinquishing their role in the collective group, which he called "race-consciousness."

Hitler was not alone in his beliefs. Nationalist political movements in Germany and Austria tended to view the state as a collective entity, describing it as a "National Community" (*Volksgemeinschaft*). More-extreme racist nationalists saw the state as a "community of the people" (*völkische Gemeinschaft*), by which they meant not just a national but a racial group imbued with a mystical sense of shared blood and common fate. In such a framework, which Hitler wholeheartedly adopted, a person mattered only for the role he or she played in serving the racial community. Hitler planned to use his power to reeducate the people along those lines by suppressing any political or spiritual loyalty beyond that to the race-nation. He would thus reclaim for Germany its place among the nations and would ensure its collective survival.

The stakes of this racial "survival of the fittest" mentality were particularly high for Hitler and for those who adopted his views, because they believed themselves to be at the top of the hierarchy but threatened with infiltration and corruption by inferior peoples. They called themselves "Aryans," although the term, in fact, refers to the language spoken by Indo-Germanic settlers from Persia and India who migrated over centuries into Europe. The Nazis perverted the word's meaning to support racist ideas by viewing those of Germanic background as prime examples of "Aryan" stock, which they considered racially superior; the typical "Aryan" in the Nazi view was blond, blue-eyed, and tall. Additionally, for Hitler and the Nazis, a racial hierarchy existed even among so-called Aryan peoples, and they dubbed those of Nordic descent, especially "Aryan" Germans, as the ultimate "Master Race," gifted above all others by virtue of innate superiority. As such, the Nazis believed they were destined to rule a vast empire they called *Das Dritte Reich*, or the Third Reich (the Nazis used this term to emphasize historical continuity—First Reich: the Holy Roman Empire of the German nation, 962–1806; Second Reich: Hohenzollern empire, 1871–1918; and the Third Reich, which would begin when the Nazi Party came to power).

Hitler painted for his countrymen a terrifying picture of this great race of "Aryan" Germans threatened with imminent danger because of the Weimar Republic's misguided leadership following World War I. By opening the doors of the nation to members of those races that the Nazis considered innately inferior and by granting them equal rights as German citizens, Hitler argued that the republic and its predecessors had encouraged intermarriage between "Aryan" Germans and inferior foreigners. This racial intermixing, in turn, produced offspring whose undesirable racial traits contaminated the purity of the "Aryan" bloodline and who were unlikely, because of their race, to be loyal to Germany. To make matters worse, the republic had also permitted the unlimited reproduction of people whom Hitler considered biologically flawed, degenerate, or a negative influence on the health of the race as a whole. This reckless lack of respect for the law of nature, Hitler argued, posed a dire threat to the purity of the "Aryan" German race and, consequently, to its very existence. "By mating again and again with other races," Hitler wrote in *Mein Kampf*, "we may raise these races from their previous cultural level to a higher stage, but we will descend forever from our own high level."

Hitler and the Nazi party outlined in clear and unequivocal terms their racial enemies. Those races included Roma (Gypsies), Slavs, African Germans, and especially Jews. Likewise, people with physical and mental disabilities, viewed as "hereditarily unfit" Germans, were deemed a biological threat to the health of the nation. As the Nazis framed it, the particular threat each so-called enemy posed to the collective whole was slightly different, but the essence was the same. Building on age-old prejudice and suspicion, Nazi rhetoric made a case for the segregation and exclusion of those whom they considered a danger to their racial purity.

In Hitler's mind, no group was more dangerous and more threatening than the Jews. Because he defined them as a race, he argued that they were instinctively driven to increase their numbers and dominate others. At the same time, he insisted that their methods of expansion were fundamentally suspect. Because Hitler tied racial continuation to territorial acquisition, he believed the Jews, who had no land of their own, should not exist at all. In fact, he theorized that when the Romans expelled the Jewish people from Israel more than 2,000 years ago and scattered them across the empire in what has come to be called the Diaspora, the Jews should have begun a long decline, ending ultimately in extinction. So why did they continue to exist and even thrive? Hitler concluded that they must have adapted to their landless environment and cultivated traits—such as cunning, deviousness, and deceitfulness—that would ensure their survival. In so doing, their very existence in his view ran counter to nature and defied the intended course of human history.

Specifically, Hitler believed that the Jews escaped extinction by migrating and attaching themselves to existing states or communities, always pushing their own interests and exploiting the native people whose territory they entered. According to Hitler, the Jewish nature was the opposite of the "Aryan" Germans' nature. Whereas the Nazis prized racial hierarchies and purity of bloodlines, the Jews, in his view, sought race-mixing, assimilation, and equality; whereas the Germans valued national strength and loyalty, the Jews weakened states by cultivating international businesses and financial institutions that fostered interdependence among nations. Hitler presented Jews as parasites, who used devious means, such as financial profiteering, media control, and race-mixing, to weaken the "host" nation, dull its race-consciousness, and reduce its capacity to defend itself. He voiced his view in a speech in Nuremberg in January 1923: "The internal expurgation of the Jewish spirit is not possible in any Platonic way, for the Jewish spirit is the product of the Jewish person. Unless we expel the Jewish people soon, they will have Judaized our people within a very short time."

Hitler believed that the Soviet Union was the first country in which the Jews had triumphed and that the Jews were using the Communist state to enslave the Slavic population. Like other Nazi leaders and right-wing nationalist politicians, he imagined that Jews were creating conditions necessary for a Soviet revolutionary takeover in Germany: massive unemployment, hunger, and homelessness. In his view, then, rather than a legitimate political and economic structure, communism was a tool devised by Jews to disguise their dominance and control of the Slav and so-called Asiatic peoples of eastern Europe and Eurasia. In the fact that two of every three European Jews lived in eastern Europe, Hitler found further corroboration for his view that the region had been infiltrated and taken over by the Jewish people.

Anti-Jewish paranoia was not original to Hitler or the Nazis. A fabricated publication called "The Protocols of the Elders of Zion"—first published in Russia in 1905—purported to document the secret plans of Jewish leaders who were conspiring to take over the world by, among other methods, controlling the international economy and the media. That work, conclusively dismissed as "clumsy plagiarism" by the London *Times* in 1921, nevertheless continued to circulate throughout Europe and the United States, thus providing support for worldwide antisemitic political movements. For Hitler, this distorted image of Jews as aggressors, quietly plotting to destabilize the state and secretly manipulating the forces that guide the government, justified and allowed preemptive action against them. As he expressed it in *Mein Kampf*, the threat was dire: "If, with the help of

the Marxist creed, the Jew conquers the nations of the world, his crown will become the funeral wreath of humanity, and once again, this planet, empty of mankind, will move through the ether as it did thousands of years ago."

Cover of a German antisemitic children's book (left), *Der Giftpilz (The Poisonous Mushroom)*, first published in Germany in 1935. This printing appeared in 1938. Even elementary schools became forums of political indoctrination and racial hatred. Nazi propaganda taught Germans to think in racist terms. GERMANY, 1938. USHMM COLLECTION

This view of Jews as Communists who had used their cunning to take over vast areas of eastern Europe fit neatly within Hitler's theories of territorial acquisition and population expansion. He contended that Germany was facing a dangerously low birth rate, largely because the lack of living space physically restricted the nation's growth. He and many other Germans blamed those problems on the Versailles Treaty, which forced Germany to give up thousands of square miles of valuable land to its neighbors, above all to Poland in the east and to France in the west. The result, as the Nazis saw it, was that Germany was losing the competition for land and population to the inferior Slavs, who occupied huge parts of the continent to the east.

To survive, Hitler argued, Germany must go to war, break the encirclement of the country by its enemies, reconquer the territory lost after World War I, and create a vast empire in the east. Despite the costs of war, the increased living space would provide Germany with the lands needed to expand its population and with the resources necessary to elevate it to world-power status. In the threatening and urgent language so characteristic of Nazism, Hitler warned that the opportunity was almost lost. If "Aryan" Germans did not act decisively, they would come under the control of the Communist Jews and, in turn, be swept away by the masses of barbaric, uncivilized Slavs to the east.

For Hitler, German conquest would also destroy—once and for all time—the enemy of all peoples: the Jews. Hitler preached a simple tautology: on the one hand, the destruction of the Jews would weaken the Soviet state and facilitate the conquest of new living space for Germany; on the other hand, the realization of Germany's natural claim to territory in the east would deal a decisive defeat to international Jewry. In the context of this ideological war against the Soviet Union, the Nazis planned and implemented the Holocaust.

Hitler's theories led to the persecution of so-called inferior races inside Germany and, following the onset of war, the subjugation of various groups throughout the new German empire. The successful realization of his ideas, however, depended on the complete coop-eration and unity of the National Community, which was to be made up of race-conscious "Aryan" Germans who accepted, obeyed, and conformed with Nazi ideology and social norms. Hitler and the Nazis demanded the public's unconditional obedience, tolerating no criticism or dissent. Indeed, they saw it as their duty to conduct a perpetual "self-purge" of society, rooting out those who failed to support their views and help realize their vision. For this reason, those who rejected Nazi ideology, even if they were considered racially pure "Aryan" Germans, found themselves in grave danger.

A German Jewish schoolboy (right) wears the compulsory yellow Star of David. BERLIN, GERMANY, 1942. USHMM, COURTESY OF YAD VASHEM PHOTO ARCHIVES

For Adolf Hitler and those who adopted his theories and embraced his views, a race-conscious government naturally needed to tend to its survival imperatives: to identify

German conquest, for Hitler,

would also destroy those he perceived

to be the enemy of all peoples: the Jews.

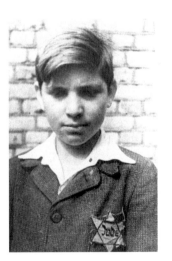

and segregate races, to subdue so-called inferior peoples and promote the reproduction of superior ones, and to go to war to seize territory from neighboring nations. Moral and legal considerations were irrelevant, Hitler cautioned, for the iron law of nature dictated that the strong take from the weak. By virtue of their racial superiority, Germans had the right—indeed the duty—to suppress and eliminate the racial threats in their midst and to seize territory from the Slavs and to repopulate it with "Aryan" Germans. By doing so, Hitler insisted, they were following their own natural instincts and serving the progress of humanity. In the end, Hitler's program of war and genocide stemmed from what he saw as a hard equation of survival: "Aryan" Germans would have to expand and dominate, a process requiring the elimination of all racial threats—especially the Jews—or else they would face extinction themselves.

ENEMIES OF THE REGIME:

Political Opponents, Jehovah's Witnesses, and Homosexuals

ADOLF HITLER, THE ONETIME STRUGGLING LEADER OF THE RADICAL FRINGE NAZI movement, was appointed Reich Chancellor of Germany by President Paul von Hindenburg on January 30, 1933. The decision came as a surprise to the nation, especially because the president was under no obligation to put Hitler in power. The Nazis—although Germany's largest political party in the national elections of 1932—did not command a majority in parliament (called the *Reichstag*) and, therefore, did not have the votes to form a government on their own. Furthermore, President von Hindenburg disliked Hitler personally and had in the past resisted naming him chancellor for fear that the move would result in a one-party dictatorship. At the same time, Hindenburg was exhausted by Germany's seemingly endless and unresolved political, economic, and constitutional crises.

Advancing in age, Hindenburg was ready to become an elder statesman, freed from the daily responsibility of governing the country. His advisers, who were close to the German Nationalist People's Party, told him that by appointing Hitler chancellor he would create a Nazi–Nationalist coalition, which would effectively end Hitler's career as a radical outsider and vocal critic of the Weimar government, stabilizing it in the process. Hindenburg was further reassured that conservative and nationalist elements in the Reichstag would use their political savvy to keep the Nazi party in check. Despite deep misgivings, the president took the fateful step, persuaded that Hitler could be controlled.

Hindenburg's advisers could not have been more wrong. Hitler and the Nazis had no intention of being managed by the president or anyone else. Indeed, with his role as chancellor secured, Hitler saw his way clear to take the troubled nation in hand. Recalling a key element of his campaign platform, he triumphantly declared the establishment of the National Community (*Volksgemeinschaft*), which the Nazis envisioned as a unified race of "Aryan" Germans under their leadership. Hitler then moved carefully—operating both inside and outside the legal framework of the constitution—to organize the police power necessary to enforce his long-term policies of racial purification and European conquest.

As a first step, the Nazis set out to crush political opposition inside Germany. In 1933, the priority enemies were the Communist and Social Democratic Parties, politicians, and trade union leaders. The Nazis began by identifying individual political opponents; branding them enemies of the German nation and dangerous obstacles to its recovery; and systematically attacking, persecuting, and suppressing them in the name of national peace.

In addition to political opponents, the Nazis identified and targeted spiritual resisters (Jehovah's Witnesses) and so-called social deviants (especially homosexuals). Nazi theory held that those people, insofar as they were "Aryan" Germans, were worthwhile members of the social order who had lost their sense of their intrinsic racial value and, in consequence, had drifted away from the National Community. German society would welcome them back, provided they embraced Nazi ideology and accepted the roles and responsibilities that came with their racial status. Although in practice the Nazis moved harshly and often with lethal outcome against activist leaders and others who resisted their authority, they expected, in accordance with their racist view, that the rank and file—perhaps after time in a concentration camp—would see the light and fall in with the collective. Those who persistently refused to be reformed were to be further terrorized and punished as a warning to other recalcitrant offenders, and, if necessary, to be removed from society.

Communists being held at gunpoint (right) by a member of the Sturmabteilung (SA) after a mass arrest of political opponents of the Nazi regime. BERLIN, GERMANY, MARCH 6, 1933. WITH PERMISSION OF THE BUNDESARCHIV

POLITICAL OPPONENTS

Hitler inaugurated his regime with a wave of public violence against political opponents. The brutality was carried out by members of the Nazi paramilitary formations, namely the SA (*Sturmabteilung*) also known as storm troopers, and the SS (*Schutzstaffel*), the elite guard of the Nazi party. On February 22, 1933, Hitler's second in command, Hermann Göring, inducted members of the SA and the SS into the police as auxiliaries, giving them

As a first step, the Nazis set out to crush

political opposition inside Germany.

license to arbitrarily beat or kill people whom they deemed to be opponents. In response to expected protests over the Nazi takeover, Göring ordered the police to shoot to kill all Communist demonstrators. In individual spontaneous acts of violence or in locally organized waves of persecution, Nazi party faithful assaulted those whom they perceived to be enemies of the regime. Street battles, such as "Bloody Sunday" in February 1933, left one Communist dead and hundreds wounded. A few months later, during a violent spree that came to be called the "Week of Blood," Nazi thugs killed dozens of political opponents in Berlin alone.

On the night of February 27–28, 1933, 24-year-old Marinus van der Lubbe, an unemployed bricklayer and recent arrival in Germany from Holland, set fire to the Reichstag, the German parliament building, in protest against Nazi persecution of the Communists. Although he acted on his own, van der Lubbe had been a member of the Communist youth movement. Hitler and Joseph Goebbels, Nazi party district leader (*Gauleiter*) of Berlin, seized the opportunity to portray the incident as being a signal for an armed Communist uprising against the state. That very night, German police arrested and detained 4,000 Communists and Social Democrats.

The following day, under the pretext of national security, Hitler—counting on the support of his Nationalist coalition partners—persuaded President von Hindenburg to issue a decree that suspended German constitutional provisions guaranteeing basic individual rights, including freedom of speech, assembly, and the press. The new law also permitted dramatically increased state and police intervention into private life, allowing officials to censor mail, listen in on phone conversations, and search private homes without either a warrant or the need to show reasonable cause. Most important, under the state of emergency established by the decree, the Nazi regime could arrest and detain people without cause and without limits on the length of incarceration. Within a few months, the German police had arrested and incarcerated more than 20,000 people in Prussia alone.

The decree provided a legal basis to intimidate, persecute, and pass discriminatory legislation against political opponents (especially those in the Communist and the Social Democratic Parties), and it offered a pretext for targeting politically active Jews. With all of the Communist representatives under arrest and after intense intimidation and bullying by the Nazis, the remaining parties represented in the Reichstag passed the Enabling Act in late March 1933. That measure gave the Nazi government the authority to pass laws and issue decrees without parliamentary consent. By divesting itself of legislative authority, the Reichstag effectively legalized a dictatorship and became a rubber stamp for the Nazi regime. By mid-July, a scant four and a half months later, the

Nazis were the only political party left in Germany. The others either had been outlawed by the government or had dissolved themselves under pressure. The government also abolished all trade unions, long the traditional supporters of leftist parties, thus forcing workers, employees, and employers instead to join the German Labor Front under Nazi leader Robert Ley.

In the months after the Nazis seized power, officials of the Secret State Police (*Gestapo*), often accompanied by members of the SA and SS, went from door to door looking for political opponents. They arrested and in some cases killed Socialists, Communists, trade union leaders, and others who had spoken out against the Nazi party. Within six months, nearly all openly organized opposition to the regime had been eliminated. Democracy in Germany was dead.

Leaders and members of the German Communist and the Social Democratic Parties and the left-wing trade unions were among the first to organize active underground resistance. Although those two parties had been rivals during the elections of the Weimar Republic, many of their members cooperated closely after the Nazis seized power. They were joined by individuals who had not been politically active before 1933 but who held socialist convictions or simply shared a desire to resist the Nazis.

Even though most of the German Communist Party leaders fled abroad or were imprisoned in 1933, remaining members met secretly and distributed illegal newspapers and leaflets produced on secret presses in Germany or smuggled in from neighboring countries. By 1935, the Gestapo had infiltrated most of the larger political opposition groups; mass arrests and trials as well as killings followed. By 1936, the regime had crushed virtually all organized left-wing opposition, including both large-scale operations and smaller resistance cells. Still, some Communist and Socialist activists continued their efforts, sabotaging the Nazis where they could and spreading their own ideals at great risk. In the end, however, they were no match for the overwhelming power of the Nazis: they never generated widespread support from the German population, nor did they seriously threaten the stability of the regime.

As part of its campaign to eliminate all potential political opponents, the Nazi regime also targeted Freemasons, made up of a variety of fraternal organizations with a long history as secret societies cultivating international connections. Using the tools of the masonry trade (the square and the compasses) to symbolize their moral and ethical ideals, many Masonic organizations had traditionally valued equality and freedom. To the Nazis, Freemasons warranted suspicion both because of their international connections (which the Nazis linked to a Jewish conspiracy) and because of their emotional ties to the French and American revolutionary movements (which also lauded both equality before the law and respect for personal freedom). Not all Masonic lodges in Germany opposed Nazi rule, however; some sought—and failed—to survive by being accommodating to the regime.

In 1935, the practice of Freemasonry was abolished, and individual Freemasons were dismissed from the civil service. Then, in April 1938, Hitler gave them partial amnesty, and in September, low-ranking Freemasons were readmitted to the civil service. Nevertheless, the Nazis continued to harass Freemasons who participated in meetings and went to lodges. Most notably, during "The Night of Broken Glass" (*Kristallnacht*), the attack on Jewish homes, synagogues, and businesses on November 9–10, 1938, SA men were encouraged to paint anti-Masonic slogans on damaged shops and synagogues. Some Freemasons perceived by the Gestapo to be engaging in subversive political activity were imprisoned in concentration camps. With only 70,000 Freemasons in Germany in 1933, they were a small minority and did not pose any real threat to the government. Still, the Nazis insisted on targeting any group—no matter how small, neutral, or benign—that espoused views contrary to those of the regime.

In the name of Germany's Communist party, I call on all class comrades, even if you have not yet joined us. If you hate fascism and love freedom, join us in the common fight. If we, the workers and working class youth, whose hands create all value, stand together, shoulder to shoulder, if we fight together, we are unbeatable. If we fight together, we will sweep up with us in the united front against fascism millions of poor farmers in the countryside, and millions of employees, civil servants, and members of the middle classes from the cities!

ERNST THÄLMANN in *Sächsische Arbeiterzeitung* on February 27, 1933

On March 3, 1933, just five days after publishing those lines, ERNST THÄLMANN (right) was arrested in Berlin. As the leader of the German Communist Party from 1925 and a one-time candidate for the German presidency, Thälmann was targeted as part of the anti-Communist crackdown that followed the Reichstag fire. He spent most of the following 11 years held in isolation in prisons and concentration camps. On Hitler's orders, the SS transferred him to Buchenwald concentration camp, where he was murdered in August 1944. GERMANY, 1932–33. WITH PERMISSION OF THE SUED-DEUTSCHER VERLAG BILDERDIENST

... Nazis insisted on targeting any group—

no matter how small, neutral, or benign—

that espoused views contrary to those of the regime.

The German authorities began establishing concentration camps soon after Hitler's appointment as chancellor in January 1933. Housed in hundreds of empty warehouses, factories, and other makeshifts sites, the facilities were portrayed as temporary detention centers for the reeducation of political opponents. The reality, however, belied such euphemistic language. Individuals were imprisoned without trial or legal recourse and held for indefinite lengths of time under conditions of exceptional cruelty. Even so, the first camps should not be confused with either the wartime concentration camps and forced labor camps, which were created to exploit the labor of their inmates, or the killing centers, which were established to mechanize mass murder. Among the original concentration camps were Oranienburg, north of Berlin; Esterwegen, near Hamburg; Dachau, northwest of Munich; and Lichtenburg, in Saxony. By the end of July 1933, almost 27,000 people—virtually all of them political prisoners—were detained throughout Germany.

By the close of 1934, the German authorities disbanded most of those makeshift facilities. In their place, the SS established a centrally organized concentration camp system. The first of the SS-run camps was established on March 20, 1933, in an abandoned World War I munitions factory outside Dachau, which is located near Munich in southeastern Germany. Dachau served as the model for what was to become a vast SS-run organization that eventually included both labor camps and the killing center at Auschwitz-Birkenau. By 1939, the system consisted of six large concentration camps: Dachau (1933), Sachsenhausen (1936), Buchenwald (1937), Flossenbürg (1938), Mauthausen (1938), and Ravensbrück (1939). The latter was to house women prisoners.

Nazi persecution of political opponents exacted a terrible price in human suffering. Between 1933 and 1939, the criminal courts, run by the Ministry of Justice, sentenced tens of thousands of Germans for so-called political crimes. Gestapo officials often seized people upon their release from prison after serving their sentences and incarcerated them in concentration camps for indefinite periods as potential enemies of the state. In Nazi Germany, once targeted by the authorities, a suspected political opponent would find no protection from the judicial system. Guilt was determined by association and suspicion, rather than by evidence and proof; likewise, once convicted, the fate of an outcast was sealed without possibility of appeal.

After 1939, as the Nazis initiated new territorial conquests and had to manage larger and more diverse groups of prisoners, they rapidly expanded the camp system both in the number of inmates and in geographic locations. Concentration camps increasingly became sites where the SS killed targeted groups of real or perceived enemies of Nazi Germany. Between 800,000 and 1,000,000 non-Jewish inmates died in the concentration camp system between 1933 and 1945. The majority of them were classified by the Gestapo as political prisoners. Like other prisoners, they were deployed at forced labor in service of state-owned, SS-owned, and private German industries. They died directly at the hands of the SS authorities or indirectly of starvation, disease, mistreatment, or accident as a result of the conditions under which they were forced to work.

JEHOVAH'S WITNESSES

The Nazis targeted Jehovah's Witnesses in Germany because they placed their loyalty to God and to their faith above any allegiance to Hitler or the state. They saw themselves as citizens of a spiritual realm, the Kingdom of Jehovah, and their faith forbade them to swear allegiance to any worldly government. In the Nazis' view, those beliefs constituted an intolerable rejection of the National Community. Few in number, the Witnesses never posed a real threat to the stability of the Nazi government. But their dedication only to God and their refusal to abandon their beliefs made them dangerous in the eyes of a regime that tolerated no rivals. For the sake of their faith, Jehovah's Witnesses faced harassment, imprisonment, and the threat of death in Nazi Germany.

The Jehovah's Witnesses (before 1931 known primarily as the International Bible Students) were first organized as a Bible study group in Allegheny, Pennsylvania, in 1872 by Charles Taze Russell. The group sent missionaries abroad to seek converts in the 1890s and opened its first branch office in Germany in 1902. Their numbers grew rapidly; by 1926, more than 22,000 Germans followed the movement, the largest association of Witnesses outside the United States. By the early 1930s, as many as 35,000 Germans (of a population of 67 million) were members or interested sympathizers of this Christian denomination.

Despite their small numbers, the Jehovah's Witnesses were relatively visible in German society. A number of their beliefs and activities—namely, door-to-door evangelizing and distribution of religious tracts—made them stand out as nonconforming outsiders. The mainstream German Lutheran and Roman Catholic churches identified the Witnesses as heretics, and many people opposed the group's efforts to win converts. Even before Hitler's rise to power, some German states and local authorities had periodically sought to limit the group's proselytizing by charging its members with illegal peddling or disturbing the peace. Local German authorities had also, from time to time, banned the denomination's religious literature, which included the booklets *The Watch Tower* and *The Golden Age*. In the early 1930s, even before assuming power in Germany, Nazi party and SA fanatics, acting outside the law, disrupted Bible study meetings and beat up individual Witnesses.

The last photo of the entire KUSSEROW FAMILY (left). Standing from left to right are SIEGFRIED, KARL-HEINZ, WOLFGANG, parents FRANZ and HILDA, ANNEMARIE, WALTRAUD, WILHELM, and HILDEGARD. Seated are PAUL-GERHARD, MAGDALENA, HANS-WERNER, and ELISABETH.

Franz and Hilda Kusserow were practicing Lutherans during the early years of their marriage, but after World War I, they became Jehovah's Witnesses and raised their 11 children in their adopted faith. After 1931, the family moved to the small town of Bad Lippspringe in western Germany, where their home became the headquarters of a new congregation.

The Kusserows endured close scrutiny by the German secret police who repeatedly searched their home and confiscated their religious literature. Firm in their conviction that their highest allegiance was to God, the family members did not bend under the pressure of harassment and intimidation. They continued to carry out their missionary work, hosting secret Bible study meetings in their home, circulating religious material, and offering refuge to fellow Witnesses.

In 1936, Hilda was arrested and imprisoned for six weeks. Not long after her return home, Franz was detained. He would spend much of the next nine years in prisons and concentration camps. In 1939, the German police took away the three youngest Kusserow children—on the grounds that their moral welfare was being threatened by their family's faith—and put them in foster homes for so-called reeducation.

The eldest child, Wilhelm (named for German Emperor Wilhelm II) refused to join the German army after the onset of World War II, adhering to the commandment against killing. For this civil disobedience, he was tried and sentenced to death and was shot by a firing squad in Münster prison on April 27, 1940. In July of the same year, his brother Karl-Heinz was arrested by the Gestapo and sent to Sachsenhausen and then Dachau. Younger brother Wolfgang also refused to be inducted into the German army. He was apprehended in December 1941 and spent months in prison before being tried and convicted. On the night before his execution, he wrote to his family, assuring them of his devotion to God. Wolfgang was beheaded by guillotine in Brandenburg prison on March 28, 1942. He was 20 years old.

Hilda, Franz, and two of their daughters, Hildegard and Magdalena, were arrested in April 1941. After serving their respective prison terms, Hilda and Magdalena were each given the opportunity to return home if they signed a statement repudiating their beliefs; they refused. They eventually found each other and Hildegard at the Ravensbrück concentration camp, where they all remained until April 1945. On a forced march from the camp, they were liberated by the Soviets. The surviving family members were reunited after the war, but Karl-Heinz, who had been imprisoned for five years, died in 1945 as a result of maltreatment during his incarceration.

BAD LIPPSPRINGE, GERMANY, CIRCA 1935. USHMM, COURTESY OF WALTRAUD AND ANNEMARIE KUSSEROW

From the outset of the Nazi regime, most Witnesses openly refused to conform. They would not raise their arms in the "Heil, Hitler!" salute; they ignored Nazi organizations such as the German Labor Front, which all German salaried workers had been compelled to join after the dissolution of the labor unions; and they failed to vote in elections or plebiscites sanctioning Hitler's government. In April 1933, four months after Hitler became chancellor, the Nazi government in Bavaria banned the regional Jehovah's Witnesses organizations. By that summer, most other German states had made it illegal for the Jehovah's Witnesses to practice their faith and to produce and distribute their literature. Twice during 1933, police occupied the Witnesses' offices and printing site in Magdeburg and confiscated religious literature. Witnesses defied Nazi prohibitions by continuing to meet and distribute their literature, often covertly. They made and shared copies of booklets smuggled into Germany, mainly from Switzerland.

The Jehovah's Witnesses came under Nazi scrutiny not only for rejecting the regime's authority but also for their alleged ties to the United States where the religion had been founded. The Nazis took their suspicions even further, linking Jehovah's Witnesses to "international Jewry," citing Witnesses' refusal to remove references to the Hebrew Bible from their publications. Although the Nazis had grievances with many of the smaller Protestant denominations on similar issues, the Witnesses were the only group that refused to swear loyalty to the state or to bear arms for its cause. Their very real resistance to the government's authority, compounded by their perceived connections to sworn enemies of the German state, made them visible targets in Nazi Germany.

Initially, the group's leaders sought to avoid a standoff with the government, sending a letter in October 1934 that explained their core beliefs and reiterated their absolute loyalty to God. They stated that Jehovah's Witnesses "have no interest in political affairs, but are wholly devoted to God's Kingdom under Christ His King." At the same time, the leaders did not shy away from firmly rejecting Nazi authority, writing the following:

There is a direct conflict between your law and God's law, and, following the lead of the faithful apostles, we ought to obey God rather than men, and this we will do (Acts 5:29). Therefore this is to advise you that at any cost we will obey God's commandments, will meet together for the study of His Word, and will worship and serve Him as He has commanded. If your government or officers do violence to us because we are obeying God, then our blood will be upon you and you will answer to Almighty God.

German authorities responded with economic and political harassment. From that date forward, Witnesses who continued to proselytize or who refused to participate in Nazi organizations lost their jobs and their unemployment and social welfare benefits; some were arrested.

The children of Jehovah's Witnesses also suffered. In some cases, teachers publicly humiliated them for refusing to give the "Heil, Hitler!" salute or to sing patriotic songs. Classmates shunned or even assaulted them, and in other instances, principals expelled them from schools. Witnesses' families were at risk because the state was empowered to judge whether parents were instilling the proper moral values in their children. The German courts ruled that it was the "task of the parents to provide their children with an upbringing that does not alienate them from German ways, raising their children in German customs and beliefs that morally and intellectually reveal the spirit of National socialism in the service of the people (*Volk*) and the National Community." German judges sometimes harshly applied a portion of the 1931 German Civil Code, which stated that child endangerment could be proven if, under parental influence, a young person behaved (or was likely to behave) in an immoral or dishonorable fashion.

Under the terms of the law, a teenager who refused to comply with Nazi norms of education, such as enrollment in the Hitler Youth, could unwittingly trigger an investigation of his or her parents. Social welfare bureaucrats could remove children from the custody of their parents on the grounds that their moral well-being was being jeopardized. In many cases, the authorities would put children in the homes of families whose beliefs reflected Nazi values; in other instances, young people were delivered into juvenile homes or correctional facilities despite having committed no crime. Parents who were Jehovah's Witnesses were forced either to inculcate in their children the beliefs that ran counter to their religious teachings or to risk losing them to the Nazi state. For their part, children found themselves facing a distinctly adult dilemma: what choice should they make when caught between love for their families and fear of punishment by the authorities? For many families, the price of remaining true to their beliefs and loyal to each other was high. From 1935 to 1938, more than 860 children were taken from their families on these grounds.

In April 1935, when the Nazi regime reintroduced military conscription, many Witnesses refused to serve or to perform war-related work. Furthermore, they tried to persuade others to ignore the summons. Although not pacifists, Jehovah's Witnesses saw themselves as soldiers in God's army and, therefore, would not bear arms for any nation. They had refused to fight in World War I, and they had been generally indifferent to the consequences of the lost war for Germany. Indeed, public memory of their passivity contributed

to hostility against them in a country still wounded by defeat and determined to reclaim its previous world stature. In response to Witnesses' disregard for the draft, the Nazi state dismissed all Jehovah's Witnesses from civil service jobs and made arrests across Germany. More than 200 men were tried by the Reich Military Court and executed for refusing military service or for undermining the integrity of the armed forces.

FRANZ WOHLFAHRT (left) was born into a Catholic family in 1920 in Köstenberg-Velden, Austria. Disillusioned with Catholicism, his parents became Jehovah's Witnesses during Franz's childhood and raised their children in their new faith.

Like other Jehovah's Witnesses, I refused to swear an oath to Hitler or to give the Hitler salute. Neighbors reported me to the police, but my boss protected me from arrest by saying that my work was needed. When the war began in September 1939, my father was arrested for opposing military service. He was executed in December. Following my twentieth birthday, I refused to be inducted into the German army. In front of hundreds of recruits and officers, I refused to salute the Nazi flag. I was arrested on March 14, 1940, and imprisoned. Later that year, I was sent to a penal camp in Germany. A new commander felt sorry for me; three times he saved me from execution between 1943 and 1945. He was impressed that I was willing to die rather than to break God's command to love our neighbor and not kill.

Franz remained in Camp Rollwald Rodgau 2 until March 24, 1945. He was liberated by U.S. forces and returned to his home in Austria. NO DATE OR PLACE GIVEN. USHMM, COURTESY OF FRANZ AND MARIA WOHLFAHRT

From 1935 onward, Jehovah's Witnesses faced renewed and intensified official discrimination. On April 1, 1935, the German government issued a national law banning the organization in Germany. In 1936, a special unit of the Gestapo began compiling a registry of all persons believed to be Jehovah's Witnesses, and informants began infiltrating Bible study meetings. In response to Nazi attacks against Witnesses, the International Society publicly supported the efforts of its brethren. At an international convention held in Lucerne, Switzerland, in September 1936, delegates from all over the world passed a resolution condemning the Nazi regime. In that text and other literature brought into Germany, writers broadly indicted the Third Reich by denouncing its oppression of Jews, Communists, and Social Democrats; criticizing its remilitarization of Germany and the nazification of its schools and universities; and condemning its assault on organized religion.

By 1939, the Nazis had incarcerated an estimated 6,000 Jehovah's Witnesses (including those from incorporated Austrian and Czech lands). In the camps, where all prisoners wore identifying badges of various shapes and colors, Witnesses were marked by purple triangular patches. Even there, they continued to meet, pray, and seek converts. They clandestinely held study groups, met for prayers, and gave lectures to other prisoners. In Buchenwald, they set up an underground printing press and distributed religious tracts. Witnesses regularly smuggled editions of their publication *The Watchtower* into the Neuengamme concentration camp in northern Germany. SS guards shot at least one Jehovah's Witness after he was caught reading *The Watchtower* and refused to denounce his beliefs.

In keeping with their overall approach toward regime offenders who were perceived as racially valuable, the Nazi authorities promised freedom from personal harm in exchange for reconciliation with the National Community. For Jehovah's Witnesses, this offer meant renouncing their loyalty to God and swearing loyalty to Hitler and the Nazi regime. In some cases, the Nazis used negative pressure by badgering or even torturing the victim; in others, they offered incentives, promising release from prison or concentration camps for those who signed a document rejecting their own teachings. The declaration read:

_____

I have come to know that the International Bible Students Association is proclaiming erroneous teachings and under the cloak of religion follows purposes hostile to the State. I have therefore left the organization entirely and made myself absolutely free from the teachings of this sect.... I will in the future esteem the laws of the State, especially in the event of war will I, with weapon in hand, defend the fatherland, and join in every way the community of the people.

_____

The vast majority of Jehovah's Witnesses won the respect of their contemporaries for refusing to repudiate their beliefs.

Conditions in Nazi camps were generally harsh for all inmates, but Witnesses were uniquely sustained by the support they gave each other and by their belief that their struggle was part of their work for God. They generally earned the high regard of their fellow inmates by their dedication and by their efforts to alleviate the sufferings of those even worse off. Individual Witnesses astounded their guards with their refusal to conform to military-type routines like roll call or the preparation of bandages for soldiers at the front. Instead, Jehovah's Witnesses sang hymns, preached to the guards, and continued to meet as best they could to sustain their emotional and spiritual strength.

Nazi persecution of Jehovah's Witnesses was not limited to Germany. Nazis targeted Witnesses throughout Europe during the course of World War II, arresting them in German-occupied Austria, Belgium, Czechoslovakia, the Netherlands, Norway, and Poland (some of them refugees from Germany) and deporting them to Dachau, Bergen-Belsen, Buchenwald, Sachsenhausen, Ravensbrück, Auschwitz, Mauthausen, and other concentration camps. At least 1,900 and possibly as many as 5,000 Jehovah's Witnesses are known to have been killed during the Nazi period. Until the liberation of the camps, those who survived continued their work among the survivors, winning converts.

HOMOSEXUALS

The Nazis' persecution of homosexual men was directly linked to their population policy and the role that they believed "Aryan" German men were to fulfill in the destiny of the Third Reich. Placing great importance on high birth rates that would expand the "Aryan" German race, the Nazis viewed men who fathered children as acting in the best interest of the National Community. Homosexual men, in contrast, were seen as degenerates whose conduct was responsible for declining birth rates in Germany. In a speech in 1937, SS leader Heinrich Himmler explicitly linked homosexuality to the fate of the nation, saying, "A people of good race which has too few children has a one-way ticket to the grave." In general, the Nazis viewed homosexuality not as a biological trait but as a behavioral choice that could be rejected or overcome. In most cases, they were prepared to accept men suspected of homosexual activity into the National Community provided that they gave up their so-called degeneracy and embraced their role as racially conscious "Aryan" Germans.

Legal sanctions against homosexuals were neither new nor unique to Nazi Germany. Since the establishment of the German Empire in 1871, sexual relations between men had been against the law. Paragraph 175 of the German criminal code declared "unnatural indecency" between men to be punishable by imprisonment of up to two years. The law did not define indecency or refer to sexual relationships between women. By the turn of the twentieth century, however, the nature of homosexuality and its inclusion in the criminal code had become a topic of medical, cultural, and political debate in Germany. Paragraph 175, reformers argued, was an unwarranted intrusion of the state into private relationships between consenting adults.

After Germany's defeat in World War I and the establishment of the democratic Weimar Republic, the social, cultural, and political climate of the country placed a greater emphasis on individual rights and personal freedom. Berlin, the nation's capital and largest city, became a center of cultural and artistic experimentation. An increased openness toward the subject of human sexuality served to make homosexuals more visible, at least in some of the larger, more cosmopolitan urban areas. By the end of the 1920s, some 350,000 homosexual men and women lived in Berlin. Scores of same-sex "friendship leagues," clubs, cafés, and dance halls provided both support and community for homosexuals. New constitutional protections such as free speech permitted an increase in advocacy for homosexual rights and publications serving their community.

KARL GORATH (right) was born on December 12, 1912, in Bad Zwischenahn, Germany. His father was a sailor, and his mother was a nurse in a local hospital. At the age of 20, Karl became a deacon in his parish church.

_____

I was 26 when my jealous lover denounced me and I was arrested at my house under Paragraph 175 of the criminal code, which defined homosexuality as an "unnatural" act. Though this law had been on the books for years, the Nazis had broadened its scope and used it as grounds to make mass arrests of homosexuals. I was imprisoned at Neuengamme concentration camp near Hamburg where the "175ers" had to wear a pink triangle.

_____

Having been trained as a nurse, he was sent from Neuengamme to work in a prisoner hospital at Wittenburg. He refused to carry out an order to decrease the food rations of Polish prisoners of war and, as a consequence, was deported to Auschwitz as a political prisoner. He was liberated from Auschwitz in 1945. NO DATE OR PLACE GIVEN. USHMM, COURTESY OF KARL GORATH

As a direct result of the broadening of traditional notions of acceptable sexuality and the increasing liberalization of German society, a number of activists began to work for legal reform. Liberal and left-wing human rights advocates campaigned to promote the civil rights of homosexuals and to repeal Paragraph 175. Dr. Magnus Hirschfeld, the founder of the Institute for Sexual Science in Berlin, for example, was a vocal critic of Paragraph 175, arguing that homosexuality was neither an illness nor a crime but a natural variation of human sexuality. Under his leadership, the institute became a symbol of the campaign for homosexual rights and legal reform in that area.

In the years of the Weimar Republic, however, some viewed the increasing civil rights for homosexuals not as progress but as evidence that German society was deserting its traditional values. They feared a cresting wave of decadence and moral abandon and responded with growing disapproval and hostility. Conservative nationalists and radical right-wing parties capitalized on this undercurrent by blaming the homosexual community for weakening established moral values and by presenting their integration into society as proof of the decadence of the Weimar Republic. As one Nazi party deputy to parliament argued in 1927, "These homosexuals should be prosecuted with all severity, because such vices will lead to the downfall of the German nation."

Identification pictures (mug shots) of a medical doctor (right) arrested as a homosexual under Paragraph 175 and deported to Auschwitz. He arrived in the camp on October 10, 1941, and died there on October 15, 1941. AUSCHWITZ, POLAND, OCTOBER 10, 1941. WITH PERMISSION OF THE NATIONAL MUSEUM OF AUSCHWITZ-BIRKENAU

After the Nazis took power in January 1933, they instituted a broad attack on so-called public indecency and moral degeneracy, capitalizing on long-standing disapproval of same-sex relationships to secure acceptance for their measures. Although the persecution of homosexual men had always had its roots in population policy, the Nazis primarily framed it for the public in eugenic terms, presenting homosexuality as a personal defect, a social vice, and a carrier of decadence that posed a threat to the well-being of the nation. They portrayed homosexuality as an infection that could become an epidemic, especially within all-male societies like the SA, the SS, the Hitler Youth, and the armed forces. The Nazis also linked homosexuality to subversive political behavior. This public message was illustrated in June 1934, when Hitler ordered the arrest and summary execution of known homosexual SA commander Ernest Röhm, together with 80 other high-ranking SA officers,

The Nazis portrayed homosexuality

as an infection that could become an epidemic.

They also linked homosexuality

to subversive political behavior.

on the false accusation that they were part of a criminal conspiracy to overthrow the government. Although Röhm's homosexuality, which Hitler had tolerated for more than a decade, was not the reason for his murder, Himmler and others focused on Röhm's sexual preference as the basis for his actions, and they used the episode to justify further attacks against homosexuals throughout Germany.

In contrast, Nazi leaders did not generally regard lesbians as a threat to their racial policies. This attitude stemmed in part from the Nazi belief that women not only were inferior to men but also were by nature dependent on them. According to this reasoning, lesbians were not particularly threatening to the regime and thus did not merit significant police attention. Furthermore, the Nazis considered that any woman, regardless of her sexual preference, could fulfill her primary role of giving birth to as many German babies as possible. Simply by becoming a mother, every woman could serve the Nazi state. Most lesbians in Germany were, therefore, able to live relatively quiet lives and were generally undisturbed by the police.

Some exceptions existed, however. Because the police in Nazi Germany regarded lesbians as antisocial—that is, as individuals who failed to conform to the norms of the state—lesbians could be arrested or sent to concentration camps. Once there, they were assigned the black triangle reserved for asocial prisoners. Although few lesbians were imprisoned as a result of their sexuality alone, the threat of persecution made living in an open same-sex relationship dangerous. Many lesbians broke off contacts with their circles of friends, and some moved to new cities where they would be unknown. Others sought the protection of outward conformity, entering marriages of convenience with male homosexual friends. Although many lesbians experienced hardships during the Third Reich, those who remained discreet and inconspicuous or who otherwise appeared to meet social expectations were generally left alone.

The Nazi crackdown on the male homosexual community began with the closing of same-sex bars and clubs and other gathering places in early 1933. Authorities soon banned their publications and closed down organizations that advocated acceptance of same-sex relationships. On May 6, 1933, Nazi student groups and sympathizers occupied the offices of the Institute for Sexual Science in Berlin. Much of the institute's library and research archives were destroyed in the public burning of books in Berlin four days later. The Nazis denounced Magnus Hirschfeld, who was in Paris at the time and who was both homosexual and a Jew, as "the Apostle of Indecency."

Prior to 1934, criminal proceedings against homosexuals had required proof that a narrowly defined sexual act had occurred. In February 1934, however, the police stepped up the surveillance of men who might be expected to violate Paragraph 175. In October, local law enforcement departments were ordered to submit to the Criminal Police (*Kriminalpolizei*, or *Kripo*) lists of men suspected of homosexual activity.

In June 1935, the Ministry of Justice revised Paragraph 175 as part of a massive rewriting of the criminal code. New language added as Paragraph 175a specifically imposed up to ten years of hard labor for "indecency" committed under coercion or with adolescents under the age of 21 or both, and for male prostitution. Moreover, ministry officials and court decisions expanded the category of "criminally indecent activities between men" to include any act that could be construed as sexual. The courts later decided that a violation of Paragraph 175 did not require a physical act; intent or thought alone sufficed for conviction. The result was a radical increase in prosecutions as the law prohibited virtually all interaction between men that was deemed sexual in nature.

Enforcement of Paragraph 175 fell to the Criminal Police. If a particular investigation had political ramifications (such as the investigation of a homosexual-rights activist for a left-wing party), the Gestapo might become involved. The police departments worked in tandem, occasionally conducting massive sweeps that primarily trapped victims from the working class. Less able to afford private apartments or homes, they found partners in semi-public places that put them at greater risk of discovery.

More often, however, the work of tracking down suspected homosexuals and arresting them depended on denunciations from ordinary citizens. Nazi propaganda that labeled homosexuals as "antisocial parasites" and "enemies of the state" inflamed already existing prejudices. Citizens turned in men, often on the flimsiest evidence, for as many reasons as there were accusations. Acting on the basis of those informants, the Gestapo and Criminal Police arbitrarily seized and questioned suspects, as well as possible corroborating witnesses. Those denounced were often forced to give up names of friends and acquaintances, thereby becoming informants themselves.

On October 26, 1936, Himmler formed the Reich Central Office for Combating Homosexuality and Abortion within the Security Police. The Nazis linked homosexuality to abortion because they believed that both obstructed the population growth that was so central to their ideology and goals. Indeed, for the Nazis, the termination of a pregnancy that might yield an "Aryan" German child was a crime equal to the refusal to father an "Aryan" German in the first place. After 1936, the Nazis instituted one national police registry for all sexual matters that they believed prevented the expansion of the "Aryan" race.

From early 1937 to mid-1939, the persecution of homosexual men in the court system reached its peak. Imprisonment was the most common punishment, but the length and type varied with the act involved and the individual's prior history. For many, incarceration

meant hard labor, part of the Nazis' so-called reeducation program. All were subjected to brutal mistreatment at the hands of police, interrogators, and guards. As word spread of the arrests and the brutal conditions in German prisons, an atmosphere of fear enveloped the homosexual community.

Despite Nazi fears that homosexuality would spread through the all-male military, the German code of military conduct did not bar homosexuals from the armed forces. With the onset of World War II, homosexuals who had been persecuted and deprived of civil rights, including some who had been convicted and imprisoned, were, nevertheless, expected to fight for their country. Homosexual conduct within the German armed forces was still prosecuted under Paragraph 175, and some 7,000 soldiers were arrested and found guilty under the law. Though sentenced to prison, those who were convicted could petition to serve in a so-called punishment battalion. During the last years of the war, German military commanders often deployed those "penal" units as cannon-fodder on hopeless combat missions.

FRIEDRICH-PAUL VON GROSZHEIM (left) was born on April 27, 1906, in Lübeck, Germany. He was 11 when his father was killed in World War I. After his mother died, he and his sister, Ina, were raised by two elderly aunts. After graduating from school, Friedrich-Paul trained to be a merchant.

_____

In January 1937, the SS arrested 230 men in Lübeck under the Nazi-revised criminal code's Paragraph 175, which outlawed homosexuality, and I was imprisoned for 10 months.... In 1938, I was rearrested, humiliated, and tortured. The Nazis finally released me, but only on the condition that I agree to be castrated. Because of the nature of my operation, I was rejected as "physically unfit" when I came up for military service in 1940. In 1943, I was arrested again, this time for being a monarchist, a supporter of the former Kaiser Wilhelm II. The Nazis imprisoned me as a political prisoner in an annex of the Neuengamme concentration camp at Lübeck.

_____

Friedrich-Paul survived his imprisonment and settled in Hamburg after the war. NO DATE OR PLACE GIVEN. USHMM, COURTESY OF FRIEDRICH-PAUL VON GROSZHEIM

The Nazis used the war as a pretext to intensify discriminatory measures against homosexual men. In July 1940, Himmler directed officers of the Criminal Police that "in [the]

future, after their release from prison, all homosexuals who have seduced more than one partner are to be placed in preventive detention at a concentration camp." This radical step, intended to stop the homosexual "contagion," meant that thousands of homosexual men convicted under Paragraph 175 whose police histories recorded multiple partners faced indefinite incarceration in the camps. Furthermore, in September 1942, the Nazi Minister of Justice agreed to transfer "habitual criminals" from ministry-run prisons to the SS-run concentration camps. Those prisoners included repeat offenders of Paragraph 175. By mutual agreement between the SS and the Ministry of Justice, the prisoners were to be subject to a process explicitly called "extermination through work."

During World War II, approximately 5,000–15,000 homosexuals were interned in SS-run concentration camps; some were required to wear a pink triangle on their prison uniforms. In addition to the extreme privations of camp existence, homosexuals in the camps were targeted in specific ways. They were often assigned to the most dangerous tasks, especially as laborers in quarries and brickyards. Attached to punishment battalions and working long hours with few breaks and often on reduced rations, many such prisoners lost their lives from exertion and from the brutality of the SS guards. Homosexual prisoners were singled out and bore especially vicious physical abuse; at the same time, they were socially shunned and sometimes abused by their fellow prisoners. They were generally isolated, occupying nearly the lowest rung in the camp prisoner hierarchy.

At the behest of German authorities, particularly the SS, physicians and scientists sought so-called medical solutions to homosexuality. Considerable disagreement existed among the professional establishment about the causes and, therefore, a recommended treatment for homosexual behavior. Some doctors considered it a genetic trait, seeking its origins within an individual's family lineage. Others believed it to be physical, but not necessarily genetic, and looked at disorders of the central nervous system or hormone levels as possible causes. And still others saw it as a mental defect brought on by a failure of character or a negative environment. Regardless of the cause, the goal throughout all the medical research into homosexuality was to find a way to "cure" it. When that failed, outright suppression of homosexual behavior became the norm.

The avenues of so-called medical inquiry, along with the underlying beliefs that gave rise to them, resulted in a chilling array of "treatments." The courts were anything but consistent: they convicted some individuals for acts deemed a result of uncontrollable compulsion, thereby forcibly committing the homosexuals to hospitals. They found others to be guilty as a result of diminished capacity or "weak-mindedness," sending those men to mental institutions and, in hundreds of cases, castrating them to suppress their sex drive. Among the men committed to psychiatric clinics, some were murdered as part of the T-4 program, which sought to rid Germany of people with physical and mental disabilities.

Homosexual concentration camp prisoners were sometimes subjected to medical experiments. For example, in late 1943, Heinrich Himmler authorized a Danish physician, SS Major Dr. Carl Vaernet, to carry out such experiments on homosexual prisoners in Buchenwald. Dr. Vaernet implanted hormone capsules in 12 male prisoners, of whom at least 10 were homosexuals. Two men died from complications of the surgery; the fates of the others are unknown.

Brutal treatment notwithstanding, the Nazi regime did not set out to kill all German homosexuals. Rather, it aimed to pressure them into changing their behavior or, if that failed, to isolate them from society and to control their supposed contagion of degeneracy. In reality, however, the Nazi state simply terrorized German homosexuals into sexual and social conformity, leaving thousands dead and shattering the lives of many more.

Using their extraordinary authority, German police arrested more than 100,000 men on suspicion of homosexual behavior. Using broad interpretations of Paragraph 175, the authorities convicted and sentenced to prison terms about 50,000 of those arrested. An unknown number of homosexual men were forced into mental hospitals or castrated rather than imprisoned. Fragmentary records indicate that at least 5,000 – 15,000 homosexual men were sent to concentration camps, a great many of whom died from starvation, disease, exhaustion, or beatings or were murdered outright.

The defeat of Nazi Germany in May 1945 brought neither reparation nor tolerance to homosexuals in Germany. The Allied Military Government of Germany, which was established in 1945 by the victorious powers to replace the central German government, repealed many decrees that had underpinned the racist and eugenic vision of the Nazis. However, the occupation authorities did not regard Paragraph 175 as a Nazi law and so left it in force after stripping it of the provisions added by the Nazis. The Allied occupation forces required some homosexuals to serve out their terms of imprisonment regardless of time spent in concentration camps. The pre-1933 version of Paragraph 175 was incorporated into the legal structure of the Federal Republic of Germany (then West Germany) and remained on the books until the decriminalization of homosexual relations between consenting adult men in 1969. The German Democratic Republic (then East Germany) reversed the law against sexual relations between men one year earlier, in 1968.

In the postwar era, German officials refused to recognize homosexuals as victims of Nazi persecution. In June 1956, West Germany declared that an individual incarcerated in a concentration camp for homosexual acts was not eligible to apply for compensation. Those homosexuals who were killed during the Nazi regime received neither commemoration nor public acknowledgment until 1985, when, in a speech marking the 40th anniversary of the end of World War II in Europe, West German president Richard von Weizsäcker explicitly mentioned the suffering and death of homosexuals under the Nazi regime. In 1994, four years after the reunification of Germany, Paragraph 175 was formally abolished from the nation's criminal code. In May 2002, the German parliament passed legislation pardoning all homosexuals convicted under Paragraph 175 during the Nazi era.

TERRITORIAL STRUGGLE IN EUROPE:
Polish and Soviet Civilians, and Soviet Prisoners of War

W HEN HITLER LOOKED EASTWARD FROM GERMANY, HE SAW VAST TERRITORY and a wealth of resources vital to the survival of the "Aryan" German race. That land was populated mainly by Slavs (defined as Poles, Russians, Belorussians, Ukrainians), so-called Asiatics (people of Turkic, Tartar, and other Central Asian ethnic groups), and Jews—all of whom Hitler regarded as innately inferior to Germans. In his mind, it was in keeping with the natural course of history for the biologically superior "Aryan" German race to seize that land and to exploit its resources and manpower to build the German Empire.

Hitler viewed Slavs as a barbaric, uncivilized horde on the verge of winning the perennial struggle for living space in Europe. He regarded the Soviet Union as a particular threat, because he viewed it as a state run by Jews who planned to take over Europe by means of a Communist revolution. For Hitler and those who shared his obsession with racial struggle, Germany had no choice but to prepare for an aggressive war to seize the territory in the east.

From a strategic standpoint, it made sense to rebuild the nation's strength, first taking over areas that were heavily populated by so-called ethnic Germans, meaning people who were culturally German but who lived outside the territorial boundaries of the Reich. Hitler began with two areas bordering on France: first occupying the Saarland, in 1935, after an election in accordance with the Versailles Treaty, and then occupying the Rhineland, in 1936, in violation of the treaty. Germany incorporated Austria in March 1938 and occupied the Sudetenland (part of Czechoslovakia) in October of the same year.

Throughout the 1930s, the major European powers appeased Hitler, in large part because they were not prepared for another world war. Publicly, they justified their actions by arguing that Nazi demands—though increasingly threatening—were aimed at regaining areas to which Germany had at least a demographic claim. The Munich Agreement of September 29, 1938, by which Italy, France, and Britain awarded to Nazi Germany the Sudetenland region of Czechoslovakia, was the epitome of this appeasement policy.

In March 1939, the Germans invaded and partitioned the rest of Czechoslovakia: they established a protectorate over the provinces of Bohemia and Moravia, set up Slovakia as a dependent state, and permitted Hungary to annex territory in the south and east of the country. Bohemia-Moravia had not been a historical part of Germany nor was it home to large numbers of ethnic Germans. Because the invasion was a direct violation of the Munich Agreement, Britain and France realized that Hitler's plans were far more sinister than they had at first appeared. Those countries resolved to go to war if Nazi Germany attacked another eastern European nation. Correctly predicting the identity of Hitler's next target, the Western powers offered a territorial guarantee to Poland within weeks of the dismemberment of Czechoslovakia.

In August 1939, Nazi Germany and the Soviet Union stunned the world by signing a nonaggression agreement (the Molotov-Ribbentrop Pact) which, in a secret addendum, called for the partition of Poland and the division of the Baltic region (including Estonia, Finland, Latvia, and Lithuania) and the eastern Balkans (Romania and Bulgaria) into respective spheres of influence. The agreement, surprising in view of Hitler's loathing for Soviet Russia, was a tactical maneuver that gave Germany the opportunity to attack and occupy much of Poland without fearing a two-front war. Furthermore, the pact called for the repatriation and settling of ethnic Germans in the new areas of the Reich, while at the same time expelling Poles from those same territories. This strategy was part and parcel of Nazi efforts to create German settlements throughout the occupied eastern territories.

THE GERMAN INVASION OF POLAND

Assured of Soviet neutrality, Hitler ordered the invasion of Poland on September 1, 1939, catapulting Europe into war. Although Polish troops fought hard against vastly better equipped German forces, the contest was not equal. After defending Warsaw fiercely and running out of food, water, and space into which to retreat, the surviving Polish units surrendered on September 27. Fighting ended in early October.

Germany directly annexed most of western Poland, where large numbers of ethnic Germans lived. The Germans formed the central and southern regions of the dismembered Polish state into a political entity called the General Government with Nazi party veteran and administrator Hans Frank as the top civilian authority.

The Soviet Union annexed the eastern provinces of Poland and, in 1940, drawing on further agreement with the Germans, incorporated all three Baltic states (Estonia, Latvia, and Lithuania) and the two eastern provinces of Romania: Bukovina and Bessarabia.

German forces hold Polish civilians (right) at gunpoint during the invasion of Poland, September 1939.

POLAND, SEPTEMBER 1939. USHMM, COURTESY OF DOKUMENTATIONSARCHIV DES ÖSTERREICHISCHEN WIDERSTANDES

For Hitler and those who shared

his obsession with racial struggle,

Germany had no choice

but to prepare for an aggressive war

to seize the territory in the east.

This partition of Poland was a prelude to a massive reengineering of the population in the areas that the Germans controlled. Like Austria, the Sudetenland, and the Protectorate of Bohemia and Moravia, the Nazis regarded most of western Poland as an extension of Germany itself. Thus, their goal for this area was complete "Germanization," thereby assimilating the new provinces politically, culturally, socially, and economically into the Reich. Above all, they envisioned a strictly German population. SS leader Heinrich Himler described the aim explicitly in the foreword to the June/July 1942 issues of the magazine *Deutsche Arbeit*, "It is not our task to Germanize in the old sense, that is, to teach the people there the German language and German law, but to see to it that only people of purely German, Germanic blood live in the East."

In contrast, the Nazis conceived of the General Government as a giant reservation for the Polish civilian population, who were to be suppressed, enslaved, and exploited for the benefit of the Germans. Kraków became the capital city because the Germans planned to turn Warsaw into a backwater town. In a top secret memorandum of May 1940 titled The "Treatment of Racial Aliens in the East," Himmler outlined the sinister plans for this part of Poland:

After a systematic implementation of these measures in the course of the next ten years, the population of the General Government will inevitably consist of a remaining inferior population, supplemented by those deported from the eastern provinces [the Polish territories annexed to Germany] and from all parts of the German Reich, who have the same racial and human characteristics.... This population will be at our disposal as leaderless laborers, and will furnish Germany annually with migrant workers and labor for special tasks (roads, quarries, construction of buildings).

The Germans wasted no time implementing their plans. Beginning in October 1939, SS and police units began to expel Poles and Jews from the German-occupied parts of Poland to the General Government. By March 1941, German authorities had evicted 465,000 people (365,000 Poles and 100,000 Jews) without warning and had plundered their property and belongings. Many elderly people and children died en route or in makeshift transit camps. The SS and police had to halt the deportations in March 1941 because the trains they were using were needed to transport soldiers and supplies to the front in preparation for the German invasion of the Soviet Union and because Governor General Frank refused to accept any more deportees.

Meanwhile, as planned, the German authorities in collaboration with Soviet leaders relocated ethnic Germans who had resided in the Baltic states, Bukovina, and Bessarabia into the homes and farms of the ousted Poles and Jews. The aim, as always, was to allow for the growth of the German population while simultaneously banishing, enslaving, or eliminating altogether so-called racial enemies and inferiors.

In addition to shifting the population in ways that suited the ideological goals of the Nazi regime, the leadership set out to dominate and exploit the Polish civilian population. To eliminate any potential for organized resistance, the Germans targeted Poland's middle and upper classes for annihilation: the intelligentsia, educated professionals, entrepreneurs, landowners, clergy, and activists in nationalist organizations. Behind the invading German troops, the SS and police deployed special action units called Mobile Killing Squads (*Einsatzgruppen*), who arrested or killed outright civilians who resisted the Germans or who were considered capable of doing so because of their position and social status.

When necessary, the SS could count on active support from units of the German army. Tens of thousands of wealthy landowners, clergymen, and members of the intelligentsia— government officials, teachers, doctors, dentists, officers, journalists, and others (both Poles and Jews)—were either shot en masse or sent to prisons and concentration camps. Army units and so-called self-defense forces composed of ethnic Germans also killed thousands of civilians. In many instances, the Germans perpetrated those murders as reprisal actions for the killing of individual Germans, for which entire communities were held responsible.

During the summer of 1940, SS and police units initiated a new roundup aimed at members of the Polish intelligentsia in the General Government. Within the framework of the euphemistically named Extraordinary Pacification Operation, they shot several thousand university professors, teachers, priests, and others. In Warsaw, the Germans perpetrated those murders in the Pawiak prison, outside the city in the Kampinos Forest near Palmiry, and in other locations.

The German conquerors targeted representatives of the Roman Catholic Church because it was a symbol of Polish nationalism (as a result of its association with the movement to reestablish the Polish state during the nineteenth century). Between 1939 and 1945, the Germans killed an estimated 3,000 members of the Polish clergy in the General Government. In those areas of Poland annexed to Germany, the Germans systematically closed houses of worship and deported, imprisoned, or killed hundreds of priests. They also shut down seminaries and convents as they persecuted monks and nuns.

The Nazis also sought to destroy Polish culture in order to keep the masses uneducated, ignorant, and, therefore, paralyzed. The Germans closed or destroyed universities, schools, museums, libraries, and scientific laboratories. They demolished hundreds of monuments to Polish national heroes. German officials decreed that the education of Polish children must end after a few years of elementary school. Himmler put the policy succinctly in his May 1940 memorandum:

———————

For the non-German population of the East, there cannot be schooling beyond the fourth grade of elementary school. The sole goal of this basic schooling is: simple arithmetic to the number 500 at most; writing one's name; and the doctrine that it is divine commandment to obey the Germans.... I do not consider reading to be necessary.

———————

Those policies dovetailed with the German occupiers' view that the Poles were valuable only as a reservoir of inexpensive manual labor. The Nazis exploited Poland's peasants and industrial workers as unskilled laborers, uprooting them from their homes and sending them—almost always against their will—to farms, factories, and labor camps throughout the Reich. There they worked for little or no wage, were subjected to humiliating measures to maintain racial segregation, and were punished brutally for perceived violations of labor discipline or fraternization with the "Aryan" German population.

In the General Government, in conjunction with an effort to "Germanize" Zamość province in 1942–43, the SS and police rounded up 110,000 Poles from 300 villages in this region. Families were torn apart when teens and adults were taken for forced labor and when elderly, young, and disabled people were moved to other localities. Tens of thousands of Poles were incarcerated in the Auschwitz and Majdanek concentration camps. Over the course of the war, the Germans deported more than a million and a half Poles, many of whom were teenagers, to work as forced laborers in the Reich.

Although Germany also used forced laborers from western Europe, the authorities imposed especially harsh discriminatory measures on Poles and, later, on civilians deported from the occupied Soviet Union. Regulations required Poles to wear identifying purple Ps sewn to their clothing and to observe a curfew; those laws forbade them the use of public transportation. Although enforcement depended on the resolve of the individual employer, Polish laborers as a rule were compelled to work longer hours for lower wages than west Europeans, and in many cities they lived in segregated barracks behind barbed wire. Social interaction with Germans outside work was strictly forbidden, and sexual relations with them constituted a crime that was punishable by death. During the war, German authorities executed hundreds of Polish men for actual and alleged sexual affairs with German women.

Poles were prisoners in nearly every concentration camp throughout German-occupied Poland and the Reich. Until 1942, Poles made up the overwhelming majority of prisoners at Auschwitz concentration camp. Whereas German political prisoners were incarcerated as punishment for nonconformity and could sometimes regain their freedom, Poles had no such status or power with which to bargain. They were rounded up, summarily imprisoned, and put to work. Unlike policy toward other "racial" enemies, such as Jews and Roma (Gypsies), the Nazis did not intend to systematically annihilate the entire Polish population, though they did seek to eliminate the leadership classes. Rather, they planned to use the Poles as a labor force and to allow the natural course of time and events—helped along by meager food rations and abysmal living conditions—to result in their gradual but inevitable demise as an independent people carrying a national culture. Malnutrition, exhaustion, and mistreatment led to an extremely high rate of death by attrition, in turn making more room for Germans to populate the region.

German authorities also executed thousands of Poles who had been "convicted" of minor offenses or violations of labor discipline; in concentration camps and some medical institutes, those authorities subjected Poles to cruel and lethal medical experiments.

In addition to German suppression of potential resisters and exploitation of the rest of the population, a cornerstone of German policy in the east was to seek and win new blood for the "Aryan" race. Himmler described it as follows in a May 1940 top secret memo on the treatment of racial aliens in the east:

Obviously in such a mixture of peoples, there will always be some racially good types. Therefore, I think that it is our duty to take their children with us, to remove them from their environment, if necessary by robbing, or stealing them. Either we win over any good blood that we can use for ourselves and give it a place in our people, or ... we destroy that blood.

According to Nazi thinking, adults could not be adopted into the race (even if they had the requisite Nordic "Aryan" blood) because they had been hopelessly Slavicized by their extended immersion in Polish culture and language. Their children, in contrast, were young, impressionable, and easily molded: to the Nazis, those Polish children represented the potential for new members of the "Master Race."

In the service of this program, Himmler planned "an annual screening of all children, ages 6 to 10, in the General Government to separate racially valuable and nonvaluable juveniles." The SS seized thousands of Polish children and considered them for possible

adoption by German parents. "If a child is recognized to be of our blood," Himmler went on, "the parents will be notified that the child will be sent to school in Germany and will remain permanently in Germany...." As promised, children who were deemed "valuable" by the Nazis were promptly taken from their parents and homes, assigned German names, forbidden to speak Polish, and sent away to be reeducated in SS or other Nazi institutions. Some of them ultimately died of hunger or disease, and few of the children who survived ever saw their parents again.

A group of Polish babies, (left) considered by the Nazis to be racially valuable because of their "German Aryan" features. They were forcibly taken from their mothers to be adopted into ethnic German families. POLAND, 1941–43. USHMM, COURTESY OF LYDIA CHAGOLL

Many more children were taken from home but ultimately rejected as unsuitable for Germanization after failing to measure up to the criteria established by SS "race experts." Those unfortunate castaways were not returned to their parents but were sent to children's homes or killed, some of them by phenol injection at Auschwitz. The Germans kidnapped an estimated 50,000 children, the majority of whom were taken from orphanages and foster homes in the annexed lands. They also abducted and Germanized infants born to Polish women working at forced labor on farms and in factories in the Reich. In contrast, if an examination of an expectant mother and the father of her unborn baby suggested that a "nonvaluable" child would result from the union, the German authorities generally forced the mother to undergo an abortion.

Within months of the Polish surrender in 1939, former soldiers and second-rank nationalist leaders, many of whom were unknown to the Germans, formed an active resistance movement whose ranks were swelled by the brutality of the occupation. Despite German efforts to quell organized opposition, the Polish resistance was one of the largest in occupied Europe: it was a virtual underground state apparatus, with more than 300 political and military groups working to subvert and sabotage the Germans. In the face of military defeat, the Polish government refused to surrender, establishing a government-in-exile in London in 1940.

Inside Poland itself, resistance groups established courts for trying collaborators and others, and they organized clandestine schools in response to the closing of educational institutions. In addition, the universities of Warsaw, Kraków, and Lwów (present-day L'viv, Ukraine) all operated underground. In December 1942, members of the Polish resistance in Warsaw formed Żegota, an organization that provided refuge, money, forged papers, and other means of support to Polish Jews. During the war, Żegota saved about 3,000 Jewish people, many of them children.

JULIAN NOGA (right) in his camp uniform, with the identifying prisoner patch bearing a P for Pole on the upper right of his jacket at Flossenbürg concentration camp. Julian was born to a Polish Catholic family in Skrzynka, Poland, on July 31, 1921. During the German occupation, Julian hid a rifle belonging to a Polish soldier but was betrayed and sent for forced labor as a farmhand for a wealthy Austrian family. He fell in love with their second-youngest daughter, Frieda, but Reich law strictly forbade romance between Germans and Poles. Julian persisted in seeing Frieda, despite repeated warnings; in September 1941, the German police arrested him and deported him to Flossenbürg concentration camp, where he was deployed at forced labor in the stone quarry.

_____

There [were] just so many, so many bad things happening in Flossenbürg. The life, daily life was terrible. You get up 4:30 ... quick, quick, quick, quick, and go to the quarry, work twelve hours, six days a week, twelve hours a day. Sunday ... Sunday before noon we do the chores, so-called, you know. Clean out your lockers, clean out the barrack, clean up yourselves, and everything. Then we had inspection, you know. If you had [a] button missing or something like that, you [were] punished for that.

_____

Julian was liberated on April 23, 1945, while on a forced march from Flossenbürg. Frieda also survived, having spent two years in Ravensbrück concentration camp. The two were reunited, and they married in 1946 and emigrated to the United States. FLOSSENBÜRG, GERMANY; AUGUST 1942–APRIL 1945. USHMM, COURTESY OF JULIAN AND FRIEDA NOGA

The Polish military also continued to fight on after the country was occupied. Officers of the regular Polish armed forces headed the underground Home Army (*Armia Krajowa*), in which they trained recruits, stockpiled weapons, and engaged in partisan operations. In

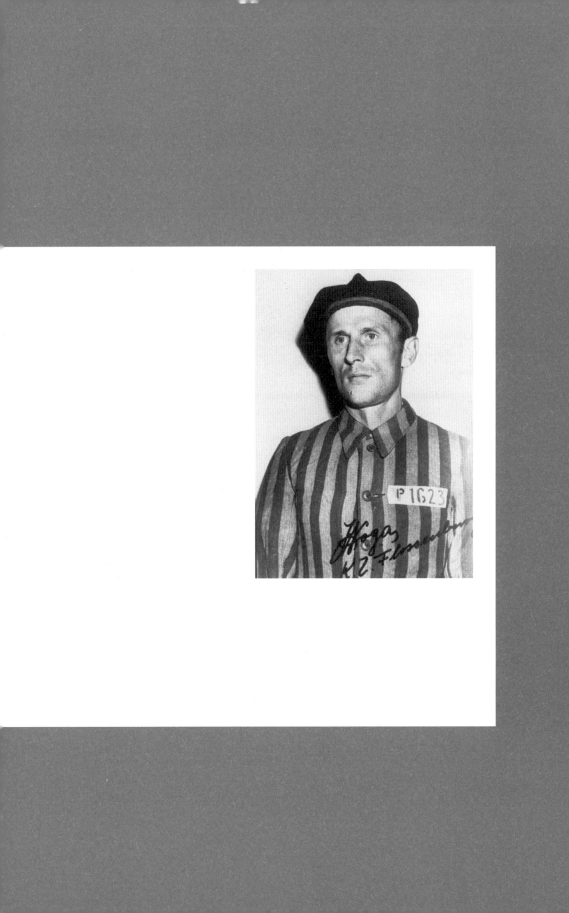

addition, the smaller Polish Communist movement organized the People's Army (*Armia Ludowa*), which also conducted partisan strikes. After the massive expulsions from the General Government in late 1942 and 1943, both Communist and non-Communist members of Polish partisan units—whose ranks were filled with terrorized peasants—attacked ethnic German settlers. The price was a heavy one, because the Germans carried out reprisals in the form of mass killings of Polish civilians. Throughout the occupation, the Germans applied a ruthless retaliation policy, destroying dozens of villages and killing men, women, and children. In the cities, public hangings and shootings were an almost daily occurrence as the Germans sought to deter Poles from engaging in further resistance.

As Soviet troops reached the east bank of the Vistula River opposite Warsaw on August 1, 1944, the Home Army launched an uprising in the capital city. After 63 days of bitter fighting (with little aid from the Soviet army), the leaders of the insurrection were forced to surrender to the Germans. Although they treated the leaders of the uprising as prisoners of war, the Germans killed or deported thousands of civilians. Acting on Hitler's orders, German forces reduced Warsaw to rubble.

Reliable statistics for the total number of Poles who died as a result of German policies do not exist; documentation on this subject is fragmentary. Most scholars estimate that close to two million non-Jewish Polish civilians lost their lives as a direct result of German occupation policies and military or antipartisan operations. Among them were Poles who were murdered in executions or who died as a result of being incarcerated in prisons, becoming part of forced labor, and being placed in concentration camps. Still others lost their lives in military battles, including an estimated 50,000 civilians killed during the German conquest of Poland in 1939; 225,000 civilians killed during the 1944 Home Army uprising in Warsaw; and an undetermined number killed in 1944–45 during the Soviet military campaign that drove the Germans out of Poland. It is important to mention, too, that the figure of nearly two million civilians does not include Poles who were victims of the 1939–41 Soviet occupation of eastern Poland and of deportations to Central Asia and Siberia. Records on that subject are incomplete, and the Soviet control of Poland for 50 years after the war has impeded independent scholarship in this area.

THE GERMAN ATTACK ON THE SOVIET UNION

On June 22, 1941, Germany launched Operation Barbarossa, an attack on the Soviet Union that violated the nonaggression pact the two countries had signed less than two years before. Within weeks, German divisions swept through the eastern part of Poland and conquered Estonia, Latvia, and Lithuania. In September, the Germans laid siege to Leningrad; by the end of October, they had captured Minsk, Smolensk, Kiev, Odesa (Odessa), and Kharkov (present-day Kharkiv). After pacifying most of the Crimean peninsula, the Germans had besieged Sevastopol. Millions of Soviet soldiers were encircled, cut off from supplies and reinforcements, and forced to surrender.

For Nazi Germany, this attack was not an ordinary military operation; it was the next step in the Nazi plan to destroy Soviet Russia (and the Jewish-Communist threat Nazis believed it contained) and to colonize eastern Europe for the expansion of the "Aryan" German race. It was the long-awaited final battle between German national socialism and Soviet communism—the decisive racial war between the Nordic peoples, led by the "Aryan" Germans, on the one hand, and the Slavs and Jews on the other hand. General Erich Hoepner, the commander of the 4th Panzer Army, outlined clearly the fundamental principles of the Nazi crusade in a memorandum dated May 1941. "The war against Russia is the inevitable result of a struggle for existence that has been forced upon us," he wrote.

It is the old fight of Germanic peoples against the Slavic peoples, the defense of European culture against the Muscovite-Asiatic flood, and the defense against Jewish Bolshevism. This war must have as its goal the destruction of today's Russia and must therefore be waged with unprecedented harshness. In conception and execution, every battle must be guided by the iron will to completely and mercilessly annihilate the enemy. In particular, the sponsors of the current Russian-Bolshevik system are not to be spared.

The Nazis approached the Soviet civilian population in much the same way as they had regarded the Poles nearly two years earlier. Their ideological position regarding both groups was fundamentally the same: Slavs were seen as _Untermenschen_, which roughly translates as "subhumans." In keeping with the Nazis' hierarchical view of racial groups, they regarded the Slavs as nothing more than useless bodies occupying land and resources that rightly belonged to the "Aryan" German race. As such, Soviet state and Communist Party officials were to be killed to prevent resistance and to stop the spread of what the Nazis considered to be "Jewish" Bolshevism.

Insofar as possible, the Germans would exploit the masses for labor; otherwise the Germans would eliminate them to make room for German settlement or expel them farther eastward, denying them essential food and shelter to survive the Russian winters. In bringing those plans to partial fruition, the Germans killed or directly caused the death of millions of Soviet civilians, deported millions more for forced labor in Germany, and enslaved still more millions in the occupied Soviet Union.

One of Germany's major war aims in the Soviet Union was the ruthless plunder of economic resources, especially agricultural produce. Hitler remembered the food shortages in Germany at the end of World War I and the resulting riots in Berlin, and he blamed them for the collapse of domestic morale. Along with other right-wing politicians, he saw a direct link between those events and Germany's eventual capitulation. In fighting *his* war, Hitler was determined to maintain civilian confidence, averting any internal crises that could lead to a repeat of those events in 1918. German planners were well aware that the spoliation of Soviet resources would inevitably result in drastic food shortages for the native population—in fact, they counted on it. In their determination to keep the German population well fed at home, Nazi leaders calculated and accepted that—as a result of this policy—as many as 30 million Soviet civilians would die of starvation.

As in Poland, the Germans crushed any show of opposition by the Soviets without mercy. Hitler's directive for the attack on the Soviet Union was specific on this point: he called on his troops to react to any type of resistance by shooting. In retaliation for partisan attacks, German forces burned whole villages and shot the rural populations of entire districts. At the same time, German military authorities made it clear that crimes committed by their soldiers were not to be punished if they were ideologically motivated. This policy was an open invitation for soldiers to behave brutally toward civilians, and it gave them not only the license but also the obligation to terrorize the population to secure the occupation and to guarantee the long-term German future.

The deeply ideological nature of the Germans' fight against the Soviet Union was reflected in the "Commissar Order" issued by the German Armed Forces High Command on June 6, 1941. Political commissars were Soviet Communist Party officials who oversaw its military units and reported directly to party leaders. Operating as they did outside the military hierarchy, commissars acted as a conduit from the party to the ranks of ordinary soldiers, transmitting political propaganda and preventing dissension. To the Germans, they represented the true "pillars of opposition," the link between the Bolshevik ideologies and the minions in the military who the Nazis believed fought blindly on Bolshevism's behalf. For that reason, German soldiers were ordered to shoot any political commissars who were taken prisoner.

The Commissar Order read: "The originators of barbaric, Asiatic methods of warfare are the political commissars.... Therefore, when captured either in battle or offering resistance, they are to be shot on principle." During the initial attack on the Soviet Union throughout the summer and autumn of 1941, the German armed forces generally complied with this order. In May 1942, however, the Commissar Order was rescinded at the urging of German field commanders, who came up against much stronger resistance when the routine shooting of the commissars became known to Soviet soldiers.

Just as the Nazis targeted political commissars as agents of the Soviet Communist Party, they regarded Soviet prisoners of war (POWs) as an integral part of the so-called Bolshevik menace. The Germans killed POWs in massive numbers, not as a result of military operations but as a part of Nazi racial policy. Indeed, the German treatment of Soviet POWs differed significantly from policy toward POWs from Britain and the United States, countries the Nazis regarded as racial equals of the Germans. Of the 231,000 British and American prisoners held by the Germans during the war, about 8,300 died in German custody. Even Polish POWs fared better; provided they were neither Jewish nor leaders of nationalist organizations, they were generally released.

The treatment of Soviet POWs by the Germans violated every standard of warfare. The Nazi regime claimed that it was under no obligation to provide for their humane care because the Soviet Union had neither ratified the 1929 Geneva Convention on Prisoners of War, nor specifically declared its commitment to the 1907 Hague Convention on the Rules of War. Technically, both nations, therefore, were bound only by the general international standard of waging war as it had developed in modern times. Yet even by that measure, prisoners of war were guaranteed certain protections. With the Soviets, however, the Nazis dropped those as well.

From the outset in August 1941, the Germans implemented a policy of mass starvation, setting a ration of just 2,200 calories per day for captured Soviet soldiers deployed at forced labor. This amount was not enough to sustain life for long, but the reality proved even worse because prisoners typically received much less than the official ration. Many prisoners received at most a ration of 700 calories a day. They were often provided as food, for example, only special "Russian" bread made from sugar beet husks and straw flour. Within a short period of time, the result of this "subsistence" ration, as the German army termed it, was death by starvation. Numerous accounts from the late summer and fall of 1941 report that the desperate POWs, suffering from malnutrition and wild with hunger, tried to ease their craving for food by eating grass and leaves.

The prisoners' suffering from starvation was compounded by a lack of decent shelter and clothing. In the makeshift camps established by the Germans, many prisoners had to dig holes in the ground to improvise shelter from the elements. In October 1941 alone, almost 5,000 Soviet soldiers died each day; by the end of the year, the prisoner population was ravaged by epidemics of typhoid and dysentery. The onset of winter accelerated the mass death because so many victims had little or no protection from the cold. POWs held in camps in the General Government were left to linger for months in trenches, dugouts, or sod houses; in occupied Belorussia (present-day Belarus), the Germans provided only pavilions (structures with roofs but no walls) to house them. Throughout the unusually

cold winter of 1941–42, starvation and disease resulted in death of staggering proportions. Between the summer of 1941 and February 1942, more than two million Soviet soldiers died as victims of the Nazi racial policy.

A column of Soviet prisoners of war under German guard (left) marches to an internment camp.
KHARKOV, [UKRAINE] USSR, CIRCA 1941. USHMM, COURTESY OF NATIONAL ARCHIVES AND RECORDS ADMINISTRATION

Many captured Soviet soldiers—especially the wounded—were scheduled to arrive at transit camps and collection centers, but instead died on the way as a result of gross neglect and inadequate provisions. Most of the prisoners caught in 1941 had to march west behind the German lines across hundreds of miles; those who were too exhausted to continue were shot where they collapsed. When the Armed Forces High Command permitted POWs to be transported by train, it provided only open freight cars and allowed days to go by without any distribution of rations. According to army reports, between 25 percent and 70 percent of the prisoners on those transports died en route to POW camps in Germany and the General Government.

The Germans not only allowed POWs to die as a result of deliberate neglect, but also shot them outright in some cases, especially those who had been wounded, because their deaths freed the German army of their care. At the urging of the German leadership, military personnel issued a directive on September 8, 1941, urging "energetic and ruthless action ... to wipe out any trace of resistance" from prisoners. Thus, they should shoot without warning any who attempted to escape. Moreover, a decree issued on September 8, 1941, stated that the use of arms against Soviet POWs was, "as a rule, to be regarded as legal," thereby providing a clear invitation for German soldiers to kill Soviet POWs with impunity.

In cooperation with the SS-led Security Police and Security Service (SD), the German army also engaged in more direct, systematic, and selective killing of groups of Soviet soldiers in the POW camps. In mid-July 1941, just weeks after the German invasion, General Hermann Reinecke, the officer in charge of prisoner-of-war affairs in the Armed Forces High Command, ordered that all Soviet POWs be screened for "politically and racially intolerable elements."

After determining through interrogation those who were "important" state and Soviet Communist Party members, intellectuals, devoted Communists, and Jews, the German camp authorities transferred those prisoners to the custody of the Security Police and SD. Once in the hands of the SS, such prisoners were shot. The SS did not carry out the killings in the POW camps or the immediate vicinity, but rather in a secure area such as a concentration camp. As many as 500,000 Soviet soldiers were shot by the Security Police and the SD by 1942. Even after the direct killing operations ceased, Soviet POWs who had been transferred to concentration camps continued to suffer under extreme and brutal oppression; the SS murdered more than 55,000 Soviet POWs in various concentration camps.

Emaciated and half-dressed outside in the winter of 1942, Soviet prisoners of war (right) stand for a picture in the Mauthausen concentration camp. MAUTHAUSEN, AUSTRIA, JANUARY 1942. USHMM, COURTESY OF DOKUMENTATIONSARCHIV DES OESTERREICHISCHEN WIDERSTANDES

In September 1941, Rudolf Höss, commandant of the Auschwitz concentration camp, conducted the first experiments of mass murder by gassing, using Zyklon B, or hydrogen cyanide, in a gas chamber constructed in Auschwitz specifically for that purpose. Höss used 600 Soviet POWs and 250 Polish civilians as victims. Beginning in the autumn of 1939, the Germans had been using carbon monoxide gas as a killing agent on people whom they considered to be disabled and who were institutionalized in Germany and Austria (see chapter 4). In those operations, the Germans found that they could kill large numbers of people in an assembly-line fashion with minimal effort and personnel. Ultimately, they would apply this technique to murder millions of European Jews.

The killing of Soviet POWs would likely have continued had the fortunes of war not changed in the winter of 1941–42. Hitler and his military planners, victims of their own ethnic and racial stereotypes, had expected a quick campaign against the Soviet Union. They viewed Slavs as dull and incompetent and believed that the Soviet Union was in the

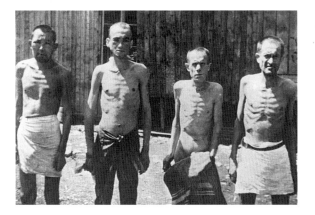

The treatment of Soviet prisoners of war by the Nazis

violated every standard of warfare.

grip of Jews, whom they regarded as cowardly and perfidious. As a result, the Germans severely miscalculated the strength and conviction of their military opponents and failed to prepare for a protracted campaign, part of which would be fought during the brutal Russian winter. The impressive initial successes of the German army only added to the German's sense of overconfidence. But as the invasion slowed and the army grew exhausted from months of campaigning, the German forces found themselves overextended, because they lacked winter clothing and equipment and had outrun their desperately needed supply lines. The Soviets began to resist more bitterly than expected, and they proved to be far better equipped than the Germans for the cold weather.

In December 1941, the Soviet Union launched a major counterattack, driving the Germans back from Moscow in chaos. Only after several weeks and tremendous losses in soldiers and equipment were the Germans able to stabilize the front east of Smolensk. Nevertheless, Hitler and the German leadership understood that the war would last much longer than anticipated. The economic requirements of a longer war and the critical labor shortage in the German economy created a desperate need for labor. In that context, the Nazi leadership realized that using Soviet POWs as laborers for the war effort was more practical than killing them. Beginning in 1942, therefore, Hitler authorized better treatment and slightly increased rations for Soviet POWs so they would have the strength to work. Although the enormous death rate among the Soviet POWs declined, it nevertheless remained higher than that among other groups of POWs. In 1943 and 1944, however, the death rates soared again as a result of starvation and disease. In total over the course of the war, the German army captured more than five and a half million Soviet POWs. Of those, more than three million died or were killed in German custody.

After the war, the ordeal of Soviet POWs who survived German captivity did not end. Soviet authorities, often without justification, tended to view returning POWs as collaborators or even traitors, because they had "allowed" themselves to be captured. After their repatriation, most POWs underwent a debriefing in which they had to justify the circumstances under which they had been caught. Some who had been liberated by British or U.S. forces had to convince the Soviet authorities that they were not Western intelligence agents. Others faced prolonged interrogation, arrest, and trial in Soviet courts. Thousands were convicted of collaboration or treason and were either executed or sentenced to confinement in a forced labor camp. Most of those who were imprisoned remained so until the death of Josef Stalin in 1953.

THE QUEST FOR RACIAL PURITY:

Germans with Mental and Physical Disabilities, African Germans, and Roma

F ROM THE MOMENT THAT HITLER TOOK POWER IN GERMANY, HE BEGAN IMPLEMENTING his vision for a new Germany—one that elevated "Aryan" Germans to the top of the Nazis' racial hierarchy and that ranked all other groups along a spectrum of relative inferiority. Nazi leaders wasted no time conceiving and adopting measures that would safeguard the "Aryan" German race, thereby ensuring that future generations would be—in their eyes—racially pure, genetically healthy, and socially productive and loyal to the state. This goal meant, above all, stigmatizing, discriminating against, and ultimately killing those whom the Nazis identified as being biologically and racially flawed. In such a context, especially Jews (see chapter 5), but also Roma (Gypsies), people with mental and physical disabilities, and African Germans, faced direct and immediate danger at the hands of the Nazis.

In time, the Nazi decision to go to war would advance those long-term goals in previously unimaginable ways. Territorial acquisition went hand in hand with population engineering as the Nazis sought to increase the number of "Aryan" Germans while simultaneously thinning the ranks of those they considered inferior by virtue of race or biology. The state of national emergency created by the war would eventually provide the pretext and cover for increasingly radical steps.

Nazi racial persecution was unique, for there was no escape—not even for those who were German by birth—from the harsh verdict of inferiority. For those who were targeted, national loyalty or communal solidarity were of no consequence: only "Aryans" who met the racial and biological standards of the Nazis could claim membership in the National Community (*Volksgemeinschaft*).

PEOPLE WITH MENTAL AND PHYSICAL DISABILITIES

The assault on mentally and physically disabled people was a central component of the Nazi quest to purify the "Aryan" race. As Hitler described it, Germany was facing "death of the race" (*Volkstod*) caused by the unchecked increase in hereditary illnesses and disabilities among the population. He presented the German people as a formerly healthy, vital race that was gradually being weakened by the ill and infirm among the populace. In the Nazi mindset, those elements within Germany's racial makeup threatened the nation's health both physically by contaminating the gene pool and economically by adding to the country's financial burdens. Using the individual human body as a metaphor for Germany, the Nazis argued that drastic measures were needed to restore the nation's racial purity, strengthen its health, and increase its productivity.

As in other arenas, the Nazis built upon strains of accepted scientific, medical, and sociological thinking, as well as contemporary prejudice, fear, and beliefs, to carry their ideology into practice. The persecution of people with disabilities had its roots in eugenics, a sociobiological theory that gained currency in the United States and Europe in the late nineteenth and early twentieth centuries. Eugenicists believed that the human race could be improved by controlled breeding and, conversely, that it could be harmed if those who were considered hereditarily impaired were permitted to reproduce. Some eugenicists feared that the genetic contamination of the human race would prevent its advancement in a host of areas, ultimately leading to the increasing degeneration of human civilization. After World War I, such ideas had been reinforced by many social planners, health care professionals, and public welfare administrators who believed that people with disabilities placed an intolerable social and economic burden on a post–World War I society in crisis.

Just as the Nazis pressured the healthy to have many children (and terrorized homosexual men in an effort to force them to father "Aryan" babies), they blamed people with disabilities for contaminating the population by having too many offspring. This two-pronged view of the racial crisis in Germany was clearly articulated in the commentary to the first law, in 1933, which affected the mentally and physically ill: "Whereas the hereditarily healthy families have for the most part adopted a policy of having only one or two children, countless numbers of inferiors and those suffering from hereditary conditions are reproducing unrestrainedly while their sick and asocial offspring burden the community."

In 1934, this 19-year-old shop clerk, (right) identified only as "Gerda D," was diagnosed as schizophrenic and sterilized at the Moabite Hospital. In 1939, she was repeatedly refused a marriage certificate because of her sterilization. BERLIN, 1933–45. WITH PERMISSION OF THE VIVANTES NETZWERK FUER GESUNDHEIT

With this justification in place and backed by scientists who legitimized their ideas, the Nazis enacted on July 14, 1933, the Law for the Prevention of Genetically Diseased Offspring. The law categorically stated that people with certain congenital (present at birth)

... Nazis pressured the healthy to have many children

... [and] blamed people with disabilities

for contaminating the population

by having too many offspring.

conditions were by definition "hereditarily diseased" and must be sterilized, although no scientific data proved that all of those ailments were inherited or transmitted across generations. The list of conditions included mental illness (schizophrenia and manic depression), retardation ("congenital feeblemindedness"), severe physical deformity, epilepsy, blindness, deafness, chronic alcoholism, and Huntington's chorea (a fatal condition that causes loss of brain function and bodily control).

The specific language of the law was unequivocal: "Anyone who is hereditarily diseased can be made infertile through surgical interventions (sterilization) if, after scientific medical evaluations, it is to be expected that the offspring will suffer severe congenital bodily or mental damage." Thus, the Nazis removed from the hands of certain individuals the most basic instinct and right of human beings—to decide whether and when to have children—and placed it firmly within the scope of state authority.

Nazi Germany was not the first or only country to sterilize people while using alleged hereditary traits as a justification. Between 1907 and 1930, as a result of laws passed in a number of individual states in the United States, more than 15,000 people were sterilized on eugenic grounds. In many cases, those operations were performed on prisoners or clients residing in mental institutions, people who neither knew nor gave their consent. Sterilization was also approved as an appropriate punishment in criminal cases after a U.S. Supreme Court decision upheld the practice in 1927. Moreover, sterilization gained support beyond eugenics circles as a means of reducing costs for institutional care and welfare for the poor.

With the onset of the Depression in 1929, sterilization rates climbed in some U.S. states. By 1939, more than 30,000 people had been sterilized in the United States, most of them in public mental hospitals or homes for "feebleminded" persons where the institution's superintendent supported the measure. Abroad, legislatures in Finland, Norway, and Sweden passed new laws permitting sterilization during the interwar years. In Great Britain, Catholic opposition blocked a proposed law.

In Germany, the massive scale of the Nazis' sterilization program far surpassed that of any other country, even as elsewhere the eugenics theories began to lose scientific support and as use of the practice peaked and began to decline. Beginning in January 1934, after the Nazis cut off scientific and social debate on the topic, German doctors carried out the compulsory sterilization of 300,000 to 400,000 people. In most cases, doctors gave "feeblemindedness"—a condition that was vague enough to include a host of mental illnesses and disabilities—as the justification for the procedure. That so many received such a generalized, unscientific diagnosis reflects the underlying fear, ignorance, and prejudice that drove this aspect of Nazi policy.

Schizophrenia and epilepsy were also commonly cited as reasons for sterilization. In 1935, the Nazis amended the law to allow for abortions in cases where the mother or father was determined to be the carrier of hereditary disease. Whereas Nazi authorities strictly prohibited abortions for healthy "Aryan" German women, they permitted and often required pregnancy terminations for those whose medical history raised concerns that a child would be born with a congenital illness or disability.

By the mid-1930s, Nazi policy grew to include within the concept of "feeblemindedness" a wide variety of behaviors that were looked down on as social ills. No longer using even the pretext of a physiological disorder, German doctors diagnosed a condition they called "moral feeblemindedness" by examining the patient's lifestyle. They assessed men and women regarding their behavior in the workplace or in public spaces. Furthermore, they judged women by their sexuality, and their real and perceived habits and practices regarding housework and child-rearing. Those Germans who failed to conform to the Nazi ideal of health and productivity—which reflected the social prejudices and mores of middle-class, suburban, and small-town German society—risked being "treated" for this subjective condition. Sixty percent of those sterilized for "moral feeblemindedness" were women.

Many of the people targeted by the 1933 law and its amendments were patients in mental hospitals and other institutions, either public or church run if they were poor, or private clinics if they were affluent. Still others lived at home, and their family doctors, social workers, and schoolteachers or directors identified them. Most were "Aryan" Germans. Doctors sterilized men by vasectomy and women through tubal ligation. In a small number of cases, physicians used X rays or radium to render their patients infertile. Of the several thousand people who died as a consequence of sterilization, women were disproportionately high among the victims because of the risks of tubal ligation surgery.

The law permitted forced sterilization under certain specific conditions, but its implementation was often arbitrary. German authorities established more than 200 so-called hereditary health courts—each with two physicians and one district judge—across Germany and later in territories annexed directly to the country. As in other areas of the German judiciary under Nazi rule, the courts provided only a pretext of due process; in fact, they tended to render routine judgments, usually without examining the patient. Most of the medical and legal community was implicated in those acts: nearly all well-known geneticists, psychiatrists, and anthropologists remaining in Germany sat on such courts at one time or another. In addition, ordinary physicians and family doctors became involved because they were required to register every known case of hereditary disease. Although courts of appeal existed, they seldom reversed decisions: occasionally, appeals courts granted exemptions to people who were deemed mentally ill but who made their livings in the creative arts and other intellectual pursuits.

The sterilization law was followed by the Marriage Law of 1935, which required that applicants for a marriage license provide ancestry and medical documentation to ensure that neither of the partners had a congenital disease or disability and that no disabled offspring would result from the union. Only those who could secure a "marriage fitness certificate" were permitted to wed. The sterilization and marriage laws worked in tandem to restrict the rights of people with mental and physical disabilities. For example, in 1934, a 19-year-old shop clerk, identified only as "Gerda D," was diagnosed as schizophrenic and sterilized at the Moabite Hospital in Berlin. Five years later, in 1939, German health authorities repeatedly refused to grant her a marriage certificate because her sterilization offered supposed proof that she had a hereditary disease.

Sterilization was not widely opposed in Germany, and only the Roman Catholic Church consistently criticized it. Most German Protestant churches, in contrast, accepted and often cooperated with the policy, allowing the nurses, doctors, and caregivers in their facilities to notify authorities of cases to which the law might apply. In particular, some Lutheran leaders greeted the sterilization law with enthusiasm, seeing in it the hope for improving the morals and ethical standards of future generations.

Not much time passed before Nazi efforts to prevent future hereditary disease escalated to attempts to eliminate it from German society altogether. In support of radicalizing their policy, Nazi leaders could cite a theoretical work titled "The Permission to Destroy Life Unworthy of Life," which was written by two German professors and published in 1920. Authors Alfred Hoche and Karl Binding argued for the validity of "euthanasia," literally "mercy death," for those who suffered from such extreme psychiatric problems or brain injury that they could be considered mentally dead. For such patients, they contended, it was both medically ethical and morally compassionate to free them from a reductive and limited existence. At the same time, they offered a binary view of the healthy versus the sick, suggesting that the existence of one was inextricably linked to the other:

If one thinks of a battlefield [in World War I] covered with thousands of dead youth and contrasts this with our institutions for the feebleminded with their solicitude for their living patients—then one would be deeply shocked by the glaring disjunction between the sacrifice of the most valuable possession of humanity on one side and on the other the greatest care of beings who are not only worthless but even manifest negative value.

The Nazis adapted the concept of "euthanasia" as put forward by Hoche and Binding and then carried it to the furthest extreme. In keeping with their absolute commitment to the National Community and their disregard of individuals' rights if those rights conflicted with the collective's rights, the Nazis pitted the well-being of the state against that of the victim. Quite simply, they saw "euthanasia" as a means of improving German society as a whole—biologically by eliminating hereditary disease and economically by freeing the nation of caring for those who were not "productive." At the same time, the Nazis were well aware that a policy of killing those with disabilities—a policy justified on such shaky ethical ground—would not find sufficient consensus among the German people. Relying on the traditional definition of euthanasia—the inducement with the permission and, if possible, the participation of the patient in a painless death for the terminally ill—the Nazis framed their actions as acts of mercy and compassion. Despite the fact that the interests of the mentally and physically ill were never of concern to the Nazis, the prevailing understanding of "mercy death" served their purposes by alleviating doubt and guilt in the minds of the German public.

The Nazis used propaganda to build public support for their policies. Popular films were especially effective in this regard. The most infamous, *I Accuse (Ich Klage an)*, which appeared in 1941, depicts a woman suffering from multiple sclerosis who begs her husband, a medical doctor, to end her life by poisoning her. He does and is then tried for murder. Throughout the film, the central act—ending the life of a terminally ill and suffering person—is portrayed as a noble sacrifice and a quasi-humanitarian act.

At the same time, the Nazis worked to instill in the public mind the idea that the nation should not bear responsibility for people who were not productive. They stigmatized the mentally and physically ill, introducing terms such as "useless eaters" and "life unworthy of life." School mathematics books posed questions such as, "The construction of a lunatic asylum costs 6 million marks. How many houses at 15,000 marks each could have been built for that amount?"

In reality, the Nazi propaganda campaign was contradictory: on the one hand mercy killing was a painful personal sacrifice undertaken in the interest of the patient; while on the other hand it was a necessary act to safeguard the economic health of the nation and biological well-being of the "Aryan" race. The Nazis sought to exploit both impulses, cultivating the human desire to protect itself at any cost to justify the killings, and alleviating potential guilt by allowing the public to see the act as a merciful one.

Those efforts notwithstanding, Nazi leaders understood that public acceptance of such killings would require the heightened consciousness of national emergency that only a war could evoke and, even then, an elaborate secrecy to conceal from and mislead a distracted population from what the regime actually intended to do. As early as 1935, Hitler had declared, when asked on one occasion, that "in the event of war, [he] would take up the question of euthanasia and enforce it" because "such a problem would be more easily solved" during wartime. Hitler expected that the upheaval of international conflict and the diminished value of human life in time of war would temper, if not mute, any opposition to "euthanasia" policy. Nevertheless, outright killings of this kind violated existing German laws against murder and assisted suicide. It also raised concerns among those in the medical profession who were essential to the entire operation.

To circumvent the legal implications and to ensure the personal protection of those who would instigate and carry out the murders, Hitler signed a secret authorization order in October 1939. Despite its secret nature, this authorization, written as it was for the future, had to convey the impression that this killing was not only compassionate for the patient but also essential for the nation, which, now that it was at war, had to conserve resources and protect its economy. Hence, the order was backdated to September 1, 1939, the day Germany invaded Poland and unleashed World War II. Indeed, many Germans who might have opposed such "mercy deaths" in peacetime came to support them, or at least to acquiesce in the need for them as a wartime measure.

In the spring and summer of 1939, with Hitler's operational order for the invasion of Poland already in place, key Nazi officials, along with numerous German medical, legal, and health care authorities, developed detailed plans for the systematic murder of people who had mental and physical disabilities and were living in institutions. As a first priority, the conspirators ironed out the details for murdering German newborns and children. In August 1939, they established the Reich Committee for the Scientific Registration of Serious Hereditary and Congenital Diseases, often called simply the Reich Committee. Under the pretext of studying hereditary disease, the Reich Committee was designed to identify and locate children deemed by medical professionals to be unworthy of life. On August 18, the Reich Ministry of the Interior ordered midwives and physicians to fill out detailed questionnaires regarding the medical condition of all children who were up to three years of age, who resided in institutions, and who appeared to have serious congenital illnesses. Within a year, officials expanded the scope of the information they required to include details of the patient's family history and other information that could be used to determine whether the child would be a long-term burden on the state.

The murder of the institutionalized children began in October 1939 after Hitler signed the previously mentioned authorization. Despite the added leeway offered by the wartime atmosphere, doctors and other health care officials, finding the strictest secrecy necessary, concocted seemingly plausible stories to deceive the children's families. For the children marked for death, they fabricated illnesses that required "treatment" and warned parents that their children might need risky but important medical procedures. They created—at least on paper—"Reich Committee Institutions" as a front for "euthanasia" killings, presenting them as special hospitals for the care and treatment of the very ill and notifying parents that their children had been transferred there for therapy. In fact, no such facilities existed; children who were slated to be murdered were sent to special wards in regular pediatric hospitals. To further support the charade, children usually remained for several weeks in their new surroundings, allegedly undergoing treatment. In this way, health care professionals, and state and local authorities laid the psychological groundwork for parents to accept news of the death of their children.

In the hospital, doctors usually administered barbiturates by mouth over several days until the child fell into a deep sleep and died, or doctors injected the drug directly, causing pneumonia and then death. In some cases, they simply allowed the child to die of starvation. Over the years of the program (which continued in various forms throughout World War II), authorities incrementally broadened the scope of those who were to be killed. Older children, those with relatively minor health problems, and eventually youngsters deemed delinquents were simply put to death. From 1939 to 1945, between 5,000 and 8,000 infants, children, and adolescents were murdered in some 30 children's wards established at state hospitals and clinics throughout Germany.

In summer 1939, concurrent with the concluding stages of planning for the so-called child euthanasia operation, Hitler authorized Führer Chancellery chief Philip Bouhler to develop concrete procedures for the murder of institutionalized adults with disabilities, an operation with the code name T-4 in reference to the street address—Tiergartenstrasse 4—of its coordinating office in Berlin. Physicians were integral to the success of the program: a significant number of them had advocated the killing solution camouflaged as "mercy killing." Now physicians and other health care professionals organized and carried out nearly all aspects of the T-4 program. They targeted adult patients in private and state mental institutions, and later in government or church-run sanatoria, psychiatric clinics, nursing and old-age homes, and public residence facilities for those with disabilities. Following the pattern of the child-killing operation, authorities ordered doctors and administrators to fill in questionnaires regarding a patient's health and capacity for work. The forms were designed to mislead the doctors who were providing the information; the abbreviated format and questions asked made respondents think the data would be used in a statistical survey.

The completed forms were, in turn, sent to three medical doctors who were expected to use them to assess the patient. No ambiguity existed about the purpose of the review.

Doctors marked each name with a red "+," meaning death, a blue "−," meaning life, or "?" for cases needing additional assessment. Those medical experts rarely examined any of the patients and typically made their decisions on the basis of the questionnaires alone. Medical authorities involved in those decisions over life and death were neither encouraged nor expected to agonize over decisions; they received huge numbers of cases to process, and short-term deadlines clearly implied that when in doubt, they should recommend the "mercy death." In this context, individuals who were determined to be "unproductive" were particularly vulnerable.

HELENE MELANIE LEBEL (right) was born on September 15, 1911, in Vienna, Austria, to a Jewish father and a Catholic mother. The elder of two daughters, Helene was raised as a Catholic in Vienna. Known affectionately as Helly, Helene loved to swim and go to the opera. After finishing her secondary education, she entered law school.

At age 19, Helene first showed signs of mental illness. Her condition worsened during 1934, and by 1935 she had to give up her law studies and her job as a legal secretary. After suffering a major breakdown, she was diagnosed as schizophrenic and placed in Vienna's Steinhof Psychiatric Hospital. Two years later, in March 1938, the Germans annexed Austria to Germany.

Helene was confined in Steinhof and was not allowed to go home even though her condition had improved. Her parents were led to believe that she would soon be released. Instead, Helene's mother was informed in August 1938 that Helene had been transferred to a hospital in Niedernhart, just across the border in Bavaria. In fact, Helene was transferred to a converted prison in Brandenburg, Germany, where she was put to death by carbon monoxide poisoning as part of the Nazi regime's policy of killing those with mental and physical disabilities.

Helene was one of almost 1,000 persons gassed that year in the Brandenburg "euthanasia" center. She was officially listed as dying in her room of "acute schizophrenic excitement." VIENNA, AUSTRIA; NO DATE GIVEN. USHMM.

At every step along the way, Nazi officials and members of the medical establishment carried out elaborate subterfuges to deceive the victims, their families, and the general public. Their method was to camouflage the killing operations by making each step in the process appear legitimate. Officials of the Charitable Foundation for the Transport of Patients Inc. (the organization created to transfer patients to killing facilities) sent lists of patients to be collected and issued instructions regarding the orderly transfer of people, medical records, and possessions. SS and police officers dressed up as doctors and nurses

Nazi officials and members of the medical establishment

carried out elaborate subterfuges to deceive

the victims, their families, and the general public.

in white coats and rode along in the buses to assuage the anxieties of those on board. To keep the public from seeing too much and raising questions, the bus windows were blacked out or covered with curtains. With such precautionary measures in place, T-4 personnel transported patients to the sanatoria where they would be put to death in gas chambers.

Within the framework of T-4, German health care officials and administrators, assisted by experts from the Criminal Police Technical Institute, established gassing installations at six existing facilities: Bernburg, Brandenburg, Grafeneck, Hadamar, Hartheim, and Sonnenstein. When the victims arrived, health care workers explained to them that they would undergo a physical evaluation and take a disinfecting shower. Lulled into a false sense of security by the seemingly routine measures, the individuals were crowded into gas chambers (disguised as showers complete with fake nozzles) and suffocated by carbon monoxide gas. Orderlies then removed the corpses from the chambers, extracted gold teeth, and burned the bodies in adjacent crematoria. Many elements of those facilities and procedures would serve as prototypes for the massive killing operations that took place in occupied Poland later in the war.

The Nazis carefully crafted their efforts to cover up the real nature of the killings, but the secrecy surrounding T-4 inevitably broke down. The German authorities could not explain away the sudden death of thousands of institutionalized but often otherwise physically healthy people, and the disturbing similarities of cause, place, and day of death in official certificates further heightened public suspicion. Frequent missteps contributed to the growing general awareness: facility workers filled urns with ashes to give to the victims' families, but hairpins turned up in the remains of male relatives; physicians falsified death certificates (and sent letters of condolences to relatives), but the cause of death was listed as appendicitis when the patient had undergone an appendectomy years before.

Word leaked out in other ways, as well: some "euthanasia" center personnel were indiscreet while drinking in local pubs after work, and, in the town of Hadamar, thick smoke coming from the hospital incinerator was said to be visible every day. School pupils in Hadamar called the gray transport buses "killing crates" and threatened each other with the taunt, "You'll end up in the Hadamar ovens!" Eventually, the "euthanasia" program became an open secret.

A handful of leaders who were in the German judicial, medical, and clerical establishments and who learned of the murders from frightened and angry parents and relatives of the victims protested overtly. Judge Lothar Kreyssig, a judge on the Orphans Court in the city of Brandenburg and legal guardian to several people with disabilities, became aware of the systematic killings when a disturbing number of his wards suddenly died shortly after transfer from facilities in his jurisdiction. Suspicion turned to outrage after the judge learned of the "euthanasia" program when he consulted with certain government officials. Thereupon, Kreyssig forbade the transfer of patients out of his jurisdiction and filed a criminal complaint for murder against the T-4 managers with the public prosecutor in Potsdam. Despite receiving assurances from the Justice Minister that Hitler himself had authorized the killings, Kreyssig refused to withdraw the criminal complaint and continued to forbid the transfer of his wards to the "euthanasia" killing centers. Finally, the regime retaliated by sending him into premature retirement.

Likewise, Karl Bonhöffer, a leading psychiatrist, and his son Dietrich, a Protestant minister who actively opposed the regime, urged churches to pressure church-administered institutions that were for people with disabilities not to release their patients to T-4 authorities. On Sunday, August 3, 1941, Catholic Bishop Clemens von Galen of Münster delivered a sermon denouncing the murder of patients with mental illness. He referred openly and explicitly to the killings, informing his listeners that he himself had brought formal charges against the police in Münster for their part in this operation. He went on to decry the regime, saying,

―――――――――

[T]hose unfortunate patients must die ... because they have become "worthless life" in the opinion of some office, based on the expert report of some commission, because according to this expert report they belong to the "unproductive national comrades."... But have they for that reason forfeited the right to life? Have you, have I the right to live only so long as we are productive, so long as we are recognized by others to be productive?

―――――――――

Galen's impassioned speech caught the attention of Hitler and the Nazi leadership and encouraged other clerics to speak out. Reluctant to punish Galen directly, for fear of turning him into a martyr, the German authorities did act against several clerics who followed his example, arresting them and sending them to concentration camps. As part of a more general program to appease Catholic leaders, Hitler ordered a halt to the gassing program on August 24, 1941. Although Galen's sermon, as well as growing public unrest about the killings, embarrassed Hitler and may have contributed to the order, the reason for the halt of the killing-center gassings was more likely that the Germans had met their initial targets. By the summer of 1941, German health care authorities had killed more than 70,000 innocent residents of institutions in the T-4 program.

The public stop order was meant to quell the fears and discomfort of the German citizenry. Even though the T-4 program had all but ended and most of its management and leadership had moved to other projects, including the mass murder of the European Jews, Hitler's order did not bring an end to the systematized murder that the regime labeled "euthanasia." Instead, German authorities continued to kill in a more decentralized process, thus involving a larger number of institutions.

The second phase of the Nazi "euthanasia" operation continued from late 1941 through the end of the war. Because of its lack of apparent centralized organization and standardized transfer and killing procedures, this phase is sometimes called "wild euthanasia." The murder of infants and small children—who had never been gassed—continued without interruption. Within months of Hitler's order, the authorities resumed killing institutionalized adults with disabilities, using lethal injections or drug overdoses at clinics throughout Germany and Austria. Many of those institutions also murdered both adults and children by deliberately starving them to death.

The Nazis would have had the German public believe that they were providing a painless death to those afflicted with incurable diseases. Yet, inside the hospitals and institutions, patients experienced neglect, abuse, and physical and psychological trauma at the hands of doctors, nurses, and other health care workers. Medical doctors brought misery to those who could have lived long lives; those same doctors failed to relieve—indeed, often exacerbated and prolonged—the agony of others who were in pain. Accounts of survivors of the killing institutions testify to just how profoundly the German doctors twisted the concept of "mercy death" and perverted the traditional medical oath to "first do no harm."

Beginning in mid-1941 and continuing until the winter of 1944–45, the Germans implemented another killing program, known under the code name Operation 14 f 13. It was, in fact, an extension of the T-4 program into the concentration camp system, which was constantly absorbing new prisoners from each German conquest. As the numbers of those unable to work increased, in part as a result of the appalling living and working conditions in the camps, SS authorities weeded them out and killed them under Operation 14 f 13. Experienced physicians from the T-4 operation were sent to perform superficial medical screenings and to review registration forms filled out by camp authorities. They then designated prisoners of all nationalities and types to be sent to the killing centers at Bernburg, Hartheim, and Sonnenstein, where the authorities had not dismantled the gas chambers. Although illness was the supposed determining factor for selection, doctors often judged prisoners on the basis of their so-called crime, racial status, and anti- or pro-German sentiment. The German authorities killed nearly 13,000 people in Operation 14 f 13.

As a general rule, the Germans were indifferent to the fate of people with disabilities in the lands they occupied. Moreover, they did not intend to feed residents of institutions and often needed the buildings and grounds for other purposes. As a result, military, SS, and police units killed tens of thousands of people who had mental and physical disabilities and who resided in institutions throughout occupied Poland and the Soviet Union. In just over one month in the fall of 1939, German SS and police shot about 3,700 institutionalized patients with mental disabilities in the region of Bydgoszcz, Poland, alone. Although regular army units did not, as a matter of policy, participate in such killing operations in Poland, some instances of their involvement have been documented. In the occupied Soviet Union, however, military units did participate in murdering institutionalized people with disabilities. Insufficient documentation exists to determine the total number of institutionalized people with disabilities whom the Germans killed in occupied Poland and the occupied Soviet Union. At a minimum, however, the victims number in the tens of thousands.

By carrying out their "euthanasia" program, German authorities got their first practical experience in using gas chambers for mass murder. Both the engineers who designed the chambers and many of the T-4 personnel who operated them were transferred to occupied Poland in the autumn of 1941 to construct killing centers. Many would later play a key role in the implementation of the mass murder of the Jews. Among those perpetrators were police officers, physicians, and other health care workers, including the former operations supervisor at Hartheim, Criminal Police Captain Christian Wirth; his colleague and successor, Franz Reichleitner, and Reichleitner's deputy, Franz Stangl; Dr. Irmfried Eberl, the chief of the Brandenburg killing center; and Gottlieb Hering, the supervisor of the gassing operations at Bernburg and Hadamar. Those infamous Nazi commandants were intimately involved in the creation and daily operations of the killing centers at Bełżec, Chełmno, Sobibór, and Treblinka.

The "euthanasia" murders continued until the last days of World War II and, indeed, expanded to include an ever-wider range of victims, including so-called asocials, geriatric patients, bombing victims, foreign forced laborers, and even permanently disabled German soldiers. Throughout, the Nazi regime continued to publicize the message that people with mental disabilities and certain physical ailments were "useless eaters" because they could not produce in the terms defined by the state. The authorities continued the killings until the last possible moment; in some of Germany's institutions, medical personnel carried on even after Allied troops had occupied surrounding areas. From 1939 to 1945, an estimated 200,000 Germans deemed "unworthy of life" were killed in the various "euthanasia" programs.

Some of the perpetrators, such as Wirth and Reichleitner, did not survive the war, and others, such as Eberl and Bouhler, committed suicide. A few, namely Viktor Brack and Dietrich Allers, were brought to trial after the war. However, the overwhelming majority of scientists, physicians, nurses, academics, and other health care professionals who advocated, implemented, and legitimized Nazi racial hygiene policies—even those who were directly involved in the killing—were neither indicted nor brought to a legal accounting for their actions. Many continued their professional careers in Germany after the war.

AFRICAN GERMANS

Germans of African descent are little-known victims of Nazi persecution, in part because of their small numbers and in part because the Nazis did not develop and carry out an organized program of annihilation against them. Consistent with attitudes toward all those whom they viewed as racially inferior, the Nazis ostracized, isolated, and, in many cases, physically harmed African Germans in an effort to segregate them from the "Aryan" population. Because the Nazis regarded anyone with "non-Aryan" blood as inferior and a threat to the purity of the race, they considered blacks—like Jews and Roma—to be less than fully human. In segregating and persecuting Germans of African descent, the Nazi leadership could draw on broad acquiescence from the German population.

Nazi attitudes toward black Africans were shaped in large measure by centuries of European colonial rule in the Americas, Africa, and Asia. The colonists shared faith in the superiority of Western civilization and in the right of white settlers to dominate indigenous peoples and cultures. The Germans' perceptions of blacks had an historical precedent in the oppression and murder of the Herero people under German colonial rule. In 1884, Germany declared a protectorate over the lands of the Herero, who were cattle herders in Southwest Africa (known today as Namibia). Calling on the rights they claimed under colonial rule, German settlers systematically seized the cattle on which the Herero depended for their livelihood. In 1903, the Herero people rose in revolt; in response, Germany sent a military force commanded by General Lothar von Trotha. With the full intention of crushing the resistance by ruthlessly annihilating the Herero people, Trotha ordered his soldiers to kill the men and to drive the women and children into the Kalahari Desert without supplies. Tens of thousands of Herero died.

When news of this order and its consequences reached Germany, Trotha was recalled, but not before the surviving Herero launched a full-scale counterattack. The German military forced the remaining Herero into detention camps, where they were used as forced laborers, a common practice under European colonial rule. Many died from overwork, malnutrition, and disease. During the years of the uprising, German forces and their native auxiliaries killed more than 60,000 Herero.

In the period between the world wars, an estimated 2,500 to 3,000 people of African descent lived in Germany. Among them were immigrants from Germany's former African colonies, including low-level indigenous officials who had worked as tax collectors and soldiers who had rendered auxiliary security service to German colonial administrations before World War I. In addition, some Africans had come to Germany during the interwar years as diplomats; businessmen; demobilized seamen; students; artisans; and entertainers, including jazz musicians, dancers, singers, and actors. This latter group of artists included a small number of African American émigrés seeking to escape harsh segregationist laws and practices in the United States. Finally, some former members of French or British colonial units who had been captured by the Germans had opted to remain in Germany after the war.

Perhaps the most visible minority group in Germany lived in western parts of the country (specifically, areas known as the Rhineland and the Ruhr). They were primarily the offspring of German women and North and Sub-Saharan African men whose liaisons were made possible by the deployment of colonial troops as occupation forces following the defeat of Germany in World War I. The Allied powers not only demilitarized the region but also occupied it for more than a decade. Most Germans, like most Europeans, harbored antiblack racist beliefs, and officials of the Weimar Republic condoned and promoted such feelings toward those colonial troops as a way of protesting the occupation. Building on existing prejudice, propaganda in the republic depicted black soldiers as carriers of venereal and other diseases and portrayed them as rapists of white German women. Nevertheless, despite all efforts at segregation, hundreds of relationships developed. Regardless of whether the partners married, children born from these liaisons were called "Rhineland Bastards." Between 500 and 800 children were born as a result of relations between Colonial soldiers and German women.

When the Nazis came to power, they named African Germans among those groups identified as a danger to "Aryan" German racial purity. In *Mein Kampf*, Hitler had complained that the "Jews ... bring the Negroes into the Rhineland always with the ... clear aim of ruining the hated white race by the necessarily resulting bastardization...." Most Germans had no direct contact with black people, and few approved of their integration into mainstream society. Because of the extent of existing popular prejudice and the ability to identify Africans and most African Germans by sight, the Nazis did not have to work very hard to convince Germans to cooperate in excluding and persecuting them. The small, isolated black minority was both vulnerable and exposed.

The Nuremberg Laws of September 1935 codified and defined racial groups in Germany: those with "Aryan" blood were protected by the law while those with so-called alien blood were relegated to second-class citizenship. Although blacks were not enumerated in the decree itself, the onslaught of restrictions against Jews that followed also applied to blacks

and other racial minorities. The laws served to reinforce and escalate their social and economic isolation. Some African Germans lost their jobs and their citizenship. German authorities excluded them from many career opportunities, including service in the military, and prevented them from attending universities. Eventually, German authorities interned many of them in prisons and concentration camps. There, they were often treated more harshly than other inmates; in some cases, they were subjected to medical experiments.

HILARIUS (LARI) GILGES (left), an African German dancer in Düsseldorf, Germany, was the son of a black man who stoked coal on a Rhine River steamship and of a white woman who worked in a textile mill. Like other African Germans born to racially mixed couples, Gilges experienced racism and prejudice from white Germans. He was politically active, joining the German Communist Youth Organization in 1926 and organizing anti-Nazi demonstrations. He also founded a political theater group in Düsseldorf and performed in cafés and bars and in the open air.

Just months after the Nazis took power in Germany in June 1933, the SS arrested Gilges, ostensibly because of his political activities. The following day, the body of 24-year-old Gilges was found under a bridge. His family was told he had been shot while trying to escape. On December 23, 2003, the city of Düsseldorf named a plaza after him, the Hilarius-Gilges-Platz in the old quarter, in honor of the first victim of the Nazis in the city. DÜSSELDORF, GERMANY, 1929–32. WITH PERMISSION OF THE MAHN UND GEDENKSTAETTE DUESSELDORF

The children of African soldiers and German women in the Rhineland were specifically targeted by the regime. Nazi measures against them were fueled not only by racial prejudice but also by the fact that the "Rhineland Bastards" were a visible symbol and painful reminder of Germany's defeat in World War I. The Gestapo created Special Commission No. 3, whose task was to locate, identify, and secretly sterilize the "mixed race" offspring of occupation forces in Germany. By 1937, the Gestapo had rounded up many of those children, who were by then teenagers, and had supervised their sterilization. According to available documents, at least 385 Rhineland children residing in and around the cities of Bonn and Köln were sterilized between 1935 and 1937. Typically, the order for the sterilization concluded that the measure was necessary because "the descendants of the child would retain the colored blood alien to the [German 'Aryan'] race." Some of the Rhineland children were also subjected to medical experiments; others mysteriously disappeared.

Not surprisingly, blacks residing in countries conquered and occupied by the Germans during World War II also suffered intense persecution. Little research has been done as to the particulars of these cases; however, a few known cases illustrate the scope of Nazi policy. Valaida Snow, a black American female jazz musician and singer, was interned in occupied Denmark and released to the United States in 1942, possibly in exchange for someone in U.S. custody whom the Germans wanted.

Josef Nassy, a black Surinamese, moved to the United States as a teenager and obtained a U.S. passport to travel to Europe in 1929. Eventually moving to Belgium, Nassy remained after the Germans occupied the country and was eventually arrested in 1942 as an enemy national after the United States entered the war. Incarcerated for seven months in a transit camp in occupied Belgium, he was transferred to Germany and interned in the camps Laufen and Tittmoning in upper Bavaria, where he survived the war.

Lionel Romney, a black American sailor in the U.S. Merchant Marine, was imprisoned in Mauthausen; his fate is unknown. Bayume Muhammed Hussein (also known as Mohamed Husen), a native of German East Africa, worked in the film industry as an actor in propaganda films with German colonial themes until his arrest on a false charge of "illegal" sexual relations with a German woman. Taken into protective custody, Hussein died in Sachsenhausen in November 1944.

The Germans also took a number of black soldiers as prisoners of war, though treatment of black soldiers in the POW camps was inconsistent. The Germans captured as many as 16,000 French African soldiers in 1940. As of July 1940, they had more than 28,700 French, British, and Belgian African prisoners of war in custody. The Germans are known to have killed between 1,500 and 3,000 French colonial soldiers upon their capture during the summer of 1940. Some Allied troops of African descent never reached the POW camps, although little information exists on their numbers and their fates. Approximately 200 black U.S. military personnel fell into the hands of the Germans after U.S. troops landed on the European continent in 1943 and 1944.

When dealing with black prisoners of war, the Germans sometimes ignored the rules of the Geneva Convention, which had been designed to regulate the conduct of war and the treatment of wounded and captured soldiers. In contrast to the general treatment of white U.S. and British POWs, the Germans worked some black POWs to death on construction projects or allowed them to die as a result of mistreatment and harsh living conditions in the camps.

ROMA (GYPSIES)

The Nazis placed Roma (Gypsies) among the groups they most despised and feared for the imagined threat they posed to "Aryan" German "racial purity." Reflecting long-held popular prejudices (in Germany and elsewhere) that judged Roma's itinerant lifestyle as violating the cultural norms of the European West, Hitler and his followers identified Roma as fundamentally antisocial and a biological source of criminal and degenerate behavior. Consequently, the Nazis hunted, persecuted, and killed them throughout Europe.

Roma have long been popularly called "Gypsies." Although today the term is considered too general and derogatory, it is still sometimes used when discussing the history of the Roma and state policies toward them. Collectively, Roma are an ethnic minority defined by language and some common customs. Within the Roma are smaller groupings known as tribes or nations. Although all Roma share the common Romany language (based on Sanskrit from classical India), particular tribes often speak in distinct dialects, the names of which they sometimes use to identify themselves. For example, in Germany and western Austria, Roma speak the Sinti dialect and are often called by that name. In eastern Europe and the Balkans, they are often referred to as Romani people or Roma. The term *Roma* has today come to include all "Gypsy" nations or tribes.

The Romani people have a long past, and historical fact has mingled with public perception to shape impressions and attitudes about them that persist to this day. They are believed to have migrated into Europe from the Punjab region of northern India between the eighth and tenth centuries C.E., although their exact origins and the cause of their exodus are unknown. Europeans referred to Roma as "Gypsies" in the mistaken belief that they came from Egypt. From the beginning of their presence among the settled populations of Europe during the late Middle Ages and Early Modern period, Roma were known for their markedly different appearance, language, customs, and way of life. Their social and cultural life was governed by a complex system of ritual purity laws, which distinguish unclean (*marime*) from pure (*wuzho*). Fundamentally distinct from the habits and norms of European society, those laws required that Roma live apart from non-Roma (*gage*). Historically, Roma have tended to be nomads and travelers, interacting with local peoples primarily in their roles as craftsmen, entertainers, seasonal laborers, or tinkerers (menders of metal pots, kettles, and utensils), although individual Romani families have led settled lives throughout Europe from at least the seventeenth century.

White Europeans scorned and persecuted Roma for centuries, regarding their itinerant lifestyle and their seemingly mystical beliefs with a mixture of fascination, suspicion, and fear. Traditionally, they accused Roma of being beggars, thieves, con artists, spies, and practitioners of magic who used their charms to lure the unsuspecting to their ruin. They also perceived Roma as being constitutionally unable to settle and hold down permanent employment, preferring to live by means of petty crime. Europeans tended to view the Romani practice of moving from place to place as further evidence that they preyed on the settled population by stealing or cheating and then moving on before they could be caught. Many insisted that Roma were dangerous outsiders who did not merit the respect or protection awarded to other members of society.

Many Roma became Christian in the course of their migrations through Persia, Asia Minor, and the Balkans. By the turn of the twentieth century, the numbers of truly nomadic Roma were on the decline in many places, although many who were considered sedentary continued to move seasonally, depending on their occupations. Others, particularly in central Europe, chose a settled lifestyle, and by the 1920s, a small, lower-middle class existed of Roma shopkeepers and some civil servants, including a number who were employed in the German postal service. Nevertheless, popular perception continued to set Roma apart as mysterious and dangerous strangers, which, in turn, seemed to justify ever-increasing restrictions against them.

A group of Romani (Gypsy) prisoners, (right) awaiting instructions from their German captors, sit in an open area near the fence in the Belżec concentration camp. Belżec, Poland, c. 1940; USHMM, COURTESY OF ARCHIWUM DOKUMENTACJI MECHANICZNEJ, WARSAW, POLAND.

In the nineteenth and early twentieth centuries, many social scientists and officials adopted beliefs about the hereditary nature of criminal behavior. Those ideas offered a seemingly plausible foundation for legal measures against Roma, who were viewed as constitutionally prone to theft and vagrancy. As early as 1899, the Bavarian Criminal Police established a central office for Gypsy Matters in Munich and created special file indices to identify all Roma in Bavaria. Although Roma were granted full rights of citi-

Many insisted that

Roma were dangerous outsiders

who did not merit the respect

or protection awarded to other members of society.

zenship in 1919 under the new Weimar Constitution, they were still subject to special, discriminatory decrees. Most notable among those was the Bavarian law of July 16, 1926, which outlined measures for "Combating Gypsies, Vagabonds, and the Work Shy." Within the scope of this law, the Bavarian state government prohibited Roma from camping in groups; it used Roma who could not prove regular employment as forced laborers for up to two years. Other German states passed similar legislation. Despite the promise of equal rights as German citizens, authorities, with strong support and some initiative from the general public, felt free to discriminate against Roma.

MARIA SAVA MOISE (left) was one of four children born to Romani parents in the capital of Moldavia in eastern Romania. The family lived in a mixed neighborhood that included Romanians and Roma. Her father made a living by singing and by working at some of the many wineries that dotted the Moldavian countryside.

My parents couldn't afford to send me to school. To help make ends meet, my sister, older brother, and I helped my mother pick grapes for a local winery. The work was seasonal, and we were contracted by the week. We worked hard and long, from 5 a.m. until evening.

When I was 16, my father was drafted by the Romanians to fight against the Soviet Union. The following year, Iasi's Gypsies were rounded up by the Romanian police and sent eastward by cattle car. When we disembarked in Transnistria, we were marched to a farm and left in open fields to die slowly. That's how my sister died. My husband, Stefan, managed to run away. By coincidence, my father's unit was stationed nearby, and on New Year's Eve of 1943, he smuggled some of us back to Romania on a troop train.

Maria survived the rest of the war in Iasi, Romania. After the war, she and her husband reunited and resettled in Iasi. NO DATE OR PLACE GIVEN. USHMM, COURTESY OF MERLE SPIEGEL

After the Nazis seized power in 1933, the plight of Roma grew dramatically worse. The July 1933 Law for the Prevention of Genetically Diseased Offspring, which permitted the coercive sterilization of people with mental and physical disabilities, affected Roma, despite the fact that the terms of the law did not specifically permit the sterilization of Roma. Instead, physicians and social workers diagnosed a disproportionate number of Roma with "feeblemindedness" and other conditions, which provided a basis for making them infertile against their will.

The September 1935 Nuremberg Race Laws did not explicitly refer to Roma, but subsequent interpretations categorized them (together with blacks and Jews) as racially distinctive minorities with "alien blood." Despite prevailing stereotypes, nearly half the Romani population was integrated into German society at this time, having abandoned an itinerant lifestyle. Many had married "Aryan" Germans. In fact, those intermarriages were of great concern to many in Germany—Nazis and non-Nazis alike—who viewed them as a sign that race-mixing was on the rise in Germany and that dangerous consequences would follow. Under the terms of the Nuremberg Race Laws, Roma were deprived of all civil rights, and intermarriage was prohibited.

Classifying and treating Roma as deviants and criminals was another tactic used by German authorities to persecute Roma. A 1933 Law against Habitual Criminals, though targeting recidivist lawbreakers and people suspected of serious violent crimes, also gave the police broader powers to arrest and incarcerate Roma and others deemed antisocial, including prostitutes, beggars, chronic alcoholics, and homeless vagrants.

In June 1936, anticipating the Olympic Games to be held in Berlin, the Ministry of the Interior issued a series of directives that were intended to keep Roma people out of sight so they would not mar the image of the city. Police in the capital were authorized to conduct raids against Roma; by July, they had arrested 600 Romani people and interned them in a municipal camp in the suburb of Marzahn. This "temporary measure" became more or less permanent. Uniformed police, aided by dogs, guarded the camp and prevented the free movement of the internees. With only three water pumps and two toilets, unsanitary conditions prevailed, facilitating the spread of contagious disease. In addition to violating their civil rights and subjecting them to the misery of camp life, the local authorities seemed deliberately to mock values deeply held by Roma by locating the camp near a sewage dump and a cemetery. Forced to reside close to sites of refuse and death, both of which were impure (*marime*) areas, the internees were unable to maintain the ritual purity laws central to their social and cultural beliefs. During the 1930s, municipal authorities established similar internment camps for Roma in cities across Germany.

Nazi efforts to isolate and oppress the Romani population were advanced by Dr. Robert Ritter, a German child psychologist turned race scientist. He had specialized in criminal biology and then directed genealogical and racial research about Roma in central Europe. In identifying the racial origins of Roma, he was faced with an ironic and vexing problem. According to Nazi terminology, Romani people were technically "Aryan," having supposedly originated in northern India. At the same time, they were viewed as racially inferior and hereditarily disposed to criminal behavior. How to reconcile the two? Ritter's working hypothesis was that although Roma had indeed come from India and hence had once been "Aryan," they had interbred with "lesser" peoples in the course of their migrations westward. This process had tainted their racial makeup, inclining them toward antisocial behavior and a criminal way of life and turning them, in Ritter's words, into "riff-raff without form and character." According to Ritter, "mixed-race" Roma were particularly dangerous because they had abandoned their itinerant lifestyle and lived in and among the settled population. Their close contact with "Aryan" Germans allowed them to poison society with restless and antisocial behavior.

Ritter's dubious research, in which he attempted to prove a link between heredity and criminality, eventually served as an instrument of and a justification for the onslaught against the Romani population in Germany. In 1936, Ritter was appointed director of the Race Hygiene and Population Biology Research Institute in the Reich Ministry of Health and was provided with both funding and access to criminal police files. Using those resources, he began systematically to collect data on all Roma residing in Germany and, later, in Austria and the Protectorate of Bohemia and Moravia. The Criminal Police facilitated those efforts by requiring all Roma to submit genealogical records. Ritter believed anyone with Romani blood constituted a danger to German society; he perceived even individuals with one mixed-race Romani grandparent as tainted. To prevent the further pollution of the purity of the German "Aryan" bloodline, Ritter argued that Roma should be segregated by sex and prohibited from marrying until after both partners had been sterilized. His aim was the eventual disappearance of a population he declared to be innately antisocial.

In December 1937, the regime issued a Basic Law on Preventive Suppression of Crime, which allowed police to issue so-called preventive detention orders. Under the pretext of stopping illegal acts from occurring, Criminal Police officials could arrest and incarcerate for an unlimited time all people whom they suspected might break the law. People under a preventive detention order were summarily imprisoned in concentration camps, which, until that time, had primarily been used for political prisoners and other perceived enemies of the regime. Because police officials typically viewed Roma as hereditary criminals or "work shy" and, therefore, antisocial, the decree authorized the incarceration of many Roma in concentration camps for indefinite periods.

In June 1938, as part of a general roundup of asocials, the German police arrested about 1,000 Roma and sent them to concentration camps at Buchenwald, Dachau, Lichtenburg, and Sachsenhausen. A year later, the police captured several thousand more Roma, imprisoning them at Dachau, Buchenwald, Mauthausen, and Ravensbrück.

In the camps, Roma were made to wear either the black triangle, the symbol for antisocial prisoners, or the green triangle, which designated them as habitual criminals. Sometimes they also wore the letter Z, which stood for *Zigeuner*, the German word for Gypsy. Nearly every concentration camp in Germany had Romani prisoners. In the concentration camps, Roma, like other prisoners, were assigned to forced labor in stone quarries, brickworks, or repair workshops. Denied adequate food and subjected to brutal forced labor, Romani prisoners often found that incarceration in a concentration camp became a death sentence. Following Germany's occupation of Alsace-Lorraine, the Czech lands, the Netherlands, and Poland, the police arrested Roma as antisocial elements or habitual criminals in those territories as well.

KARL STOJKA (right) was the fourth of six children born to Roman Catholic Romani parents in the village of Wampersdorf in eastern Austria. The Stojkas belonged to a tribe of the Lowara Roma, who made their living as itinerant horse traders. They lived in a traveling family wagon and spent winters in Austria's capital of Vienna. Karl's ancestors had lived in Austria for more than 200 years.

I grew up used to freedom, travel, and hard work. In March 1938, our wagon was parked for the winter in a Vienna campground, when Germany annexed Austria just before my seventh birthday. The Germans ordered us to stay put. My parents converted our wagon into a wooden house, but I wasn't used to having permanent walls around me. My father and oldest sister began working in a factory, and I started grade school.

By 1943, my family had been deported to a Nazi camp in Birkenau for thousands of Gypsies. Now we were enclosed by barbed wire. By August 1944, only 2,000 Gypsies were left alive; 918 of us were put on a transport to Buchenwald to do forced labor. There the Germans decided that 200 of us were incapable of working and were to be sent back to Birkenau. I was one of them; they thought I was too young. But my brother and uncle insisted that I was 14 but a dwarf. I got to stay. The rest were returned to be gassed.

Karl was later deported to the Flossenbürg concentration camp. He was freed near Roetz, Germany, by American troops on April 24, 1945. After the war, he returned to Vienna. NO DATE OR PLACE GIVEN. USHMM, COURTESY OF KARL STOJKA

Roma were made to wear either the black triangle,

the symbol for antisocial prisoners, or the green triangle,

which designated them as habitual criminals.

German physicians also used Roma concentration camp prisoners in medical experiments. For example, in 1944, the German air force sponsored an experiment on the potability of sea water. The SS selected 44 Roma, previously in good health, who had just been transferred to Buchenwald from Auschwitz and brought them to Dachau. The prisoners were forced to drink sea water and soon exhibited signs of starvation and severe thirst. As they became incoherent, they were physically restrained. When they were approaching death, SS doctors injected them with an experimental substance that was thought to counteract the effects of drinking sea water. Only the fact that other prisoners smuggled food and water to them enabled the Romani test subjects to survive.

In January 1944, SS doctors transferred 100 Romani prisoners from Auschwitz to the Natzweiler-Struthof camp in eastern France for use in typhus experiments. The Roma were infected with typhus bacillus and, naturally, developed high fevers, although none of them died. Later, some of those same Romani prisoners were used in gas experiments at the University of Strasbourg, in which they were injected with a so-called protective element and then subjected to various concentrations of phosgene gas. Four of the Romani prisoners died as a result of the experiments. In Ravensbrück, SS Dr. Carl Clauberg used Romani women and girls, some of them as young as eight, in sterilization experiments. As late as February 1945, approximately 140 Romani women were sterilized there. Some of the operations were performed without anesthesia, and at least ten of the women died.

After Germany incorporated Austria into the Reich in March 1938, the police established two internment camps for Roma there. One opened in Salzburg in October 1939, housing 80 to 400 Roma; the second opened in Lackenback, southeast of Vienna, in November 1940 and held 4,000 prisoners. Conditions at the Lackenback camp were particularly bad, which led to a high death rate at that camp through the end of the war.

The actions against Roma between 1935 and 1938, particularly their registration and incarceration in municipal camps and then in concentration camps, were a prelude to further actions envisioned by the Nazi leadership. Indeed, on the basis of Ritter's "race-biological" research, SS and police chief Heinrich Himmler recommended the full-scale segregation of Roma in his decree of December 8, 1938, on "Combating the Gypsy Plague." He ordered the registration of all Roma above the age of six years and their classification into three racial groupings: Gypsy, Gypsy mixed race, and those leading a nomadic and Gypsy-like lifestyle. Himmler stated that the aim of this measure was to "defend the homogeneity of the German nation" and the "physical separation of Gypsydom from the German nation." The information that Ritter and his associates gathered was essential to the police actions against Roma in Germany. In short, they provided the information necessary for the police to identify and locate Roma, and then to deport and ultimately kill them.

In 1939, some 30,000 to 35,000 Roma lived in the Greater German Reich (Germany, Austria, and the Czech provinces of Bohemia and Moravia). As in the case of other groups, the Nazi regime used the onset of war in September 1939 to radicalize its policy toward Roma. Thus, just three weeks after the beginning of the war, on September 21, 1939, German officials discussed the deportation of 30,000 Roma from Germany and Austria to occupied Poland, together with the removal of the Jews.

The experience of Roma who were sent east and murdered in massive numbers there closely paralleled the systematic deportations and killings of Jews, even though the number of Roma killed and the scope of Nazi efforts did not. The banishment of the German Romani population began in May 1940 with the transport of almost 3,000 men, women, and children to Lublin in occupied Poland. In early November 1941, 5,000 Austrian Roma were deported to Łódź ghetto. Two months later, they were sent to the nearby Chełmno killing center, where they were among the first to be killed by carbon monoxide poisoning in mobile gas vans. Similarly, in the summer of 1942, SS and police officials deported German and Polish Roma who had been imprisoned in the Warsaw ghetto to Treblinka, where they were put to death by gas. German Roma were also deported to ghettos in Białystok, Kraków, and Radom.

In a decree of December 16, 1942, Himmler ordered the deportation of the remaining pure and mixed-race Roma from the Greater German Reich to the Auschwitz-Birkenau killing center in occupied Poland. Although a change of heart prompted by Ritter's research led Himmler to permit certain exemptions for families that could demonstrate they had never intermarried through the generations, those exemptions were sometimes ignored. Even German army soldiers of Roma descent were seized and deported as Roma while home on leave. The SS and police deported nearly 21,000 Roma to Birkenau in the first half of 1943. Police also deported small numbers of Roma from Belgium, France, Hungary, the Netherlands, Norway, Poland, and Yugoslavia.

At Auschwitz-Birkenau, the SS set up a Gypsy Family Camp in Section B-IIe of Birkenau. There, Roma were held together in families because the SS leadership had not yet decided what their fate should be. During the 17 months in which the Gypsy Family Camp existed, the majority of Roma died as a result of starvation, exhaustion, and disease. To add to their misery, some Roma at Auschwitz, including children, perished as a result of medical experiments performed by Dr. Josef Mengele and other SS physicians.

In mid-May 1944, the SS tried to liquidate the Gypsy Family Camp. The Romani prisoners, apparently warned by the SS guard who was responsible for the Gypsy camp and who opposed the operation, armed themselves with improvised weapons, including knives fashioned out of scrap metal, clubs, and rocks; they refused to come out of their barracks. The SS refrained from carrying out the action at that time, and the Romani prisoners' defiance may have helped postpone their demise. However, on August 2–3, 1944, the SS destroyed the Gypsy camp at Birkenau and used the gas chambers to murder the nearly 3,000 remaining men, women, and children.

As with all so-called racial enemies of the Nazi regime, German SS and police units extended the killing of Roma into German-occupied eastern Europe. After Germany invaded the Soviet Union in June 1941, the Mobile Killing Squads (*Einsatzgruppen*), Order Police battalions, and indigenous collaborators began shooting Roma together with Jews. On so-called racial grounds, they killed tens of thousands of Romani men, women, and children in those massacres.

In western and southern Europe, the fate of Roma varied from country to country depending on local circumstances. In France, authorities had placed restrictions on the movement of Roma even before the German invasion. In northern France in October 1940, the German military commander ordered the arrest and internment of all Roma in the occupied zone. French authorities did not shrink from implementing this order; indeed, they participated in the roundups and served as guards in the camps. A number of the Roma incarcerated in camps in both occupied and unoccupied France died of starvation and disease; many others were eventually released during the war.

The German authorities deported 360 Roma from Belgium and northern France to Auschwitz-Birkenau in January 1944; 121 Belgian Roma were registered at Auschwitz; only 13 survived the war. From Holland, where, as in Belgium, itinerant Roma were subject to discrimination and persecution, the SS and police deported 245 persons designated as Gypsies from Westerbork to Auschwitz, where the SS classified them as "Polish Gypsies" in the camp records. In Italy, the Fascist dictatorship interned some itinerant Roma after 1938, although the Italian police released many of them after the fall of Mussolini in July 1943. Some joined the Italian resistance after the German occupation in September 1943; German forces killed as many as 2,000 Italian Roma in occupied Italy.

In the German puppet state of Croatia, Ustaša, Croatian fascists, killed between 26,000 and 30,000 Roma, between 8,000 and 15,000 of them in the Jasenovac concentration camp system. In occupied Serbia, German soldiers and SS units shot Roma and Jews in reprisal for partisan attacks against the military; the ratio was 50 to 100 people for every German soldier killed. Estimated numbers of Roma killed in Serbia range widely, between 1,000 and 20,000. For Greece and Bulgaria, the numbers also vary, with about 200 Roma killed in Greece and perhaps as many as 5,000 in Bulgaria. In Slovakia, although itinerant Roma were subject to persecution by the so-called Slovak Republic, few were killed before the Germans invaded the country in August 1944 to quell an uprising. In the aftermath of fighting, German forces and Slovak collaborators shot between 200 and 500 Roma.

The Romanian government deported approximately 26,000 Roma to Romanian-occupied Transnistria in Ukraine. How many died there at the hands of the Romanian authorities is impossible to pin down, but estimates range from 13,000 to 19,000. Most died as a result of disease, starvation, and brutal treatment. A post–World War II Romanian war crimes commission found that a total of 36,000 Romanian Roma were killed in Romania proper and the areas under its occupation. In Hungary, after the fascist Arrow Cross seized power with German assistance in October 1944, police forces deported as many as 28,000 Roma. The present state of documentation does not permit a firm estimate of how many died. Existing estimates range between 1,000 and 50,000; the estimate of the Hungarian War Victims Association of at least 25,000 Roma killed is probably the most accurate.

Scholars estimate that at least 200,000 and perhaps many more Roma were murdered throughout Europe during the Holocaust era. Those who managed to survive the war found that they were no more welcome after the war than before in most European countries. Few knew or cared that the Nazis had singled them out for abuse and murder. In fact, discrimination against Roma continued when the Federal Republic of Germany (then West Germany) decided that all measures taken against Roma before 1943 were legitimate policies of state and were not subject to restitution. Incarceration, sterilization, and even deportation were regarded as legitimate policies.

After the establishment of the Federal Republic of Germany in 1949, German courts agreed to compensate Roma for Nazi racial persecution but only for policies that targeted Roma and were enacted after 1943, that is, for their deportation and murder. In the early 1960s, the Federal German Supreme Court revised its position and set the eligibility date for compensation back to 1938, the date when Himmler issued his decree on the Regulation of the Gypsy Question. Nevertheless, many Roma had been incarcerated in concentration camps before 1938 for alleged crimes or asocial behavior, which made successfully claiming compensation for injuries done to them under the Nazi regime exceedingly difficult in German courts.

The Bavarian criminal police took over Robert Ritter's research files, including his registry of Roma in Germany. Ritter himself retained his credentials and returned to his former work in child psychology. Efforts to bring Dr. Ritter to trial for complicity in the killing of Roma ended with his death in 1950.

In 1982, German chancellor Helmut Kohl formally recognized the fact of the Nazi persecution of Roma. By then, most of the Roma eligible for restitution under German law had already died. Subjected to brutal suffering and mass murder during the Nazi regime and denied recognition and restitution in its wake, the Romani term for their own experience under the Nazis is *Porrajmos* (the Devouring). Discrimination against Roma did not end with Germany's acknowledgment of their suffering. Indeed, as late as the 1990s, Roma faced physical violence in Romania and the Czech Republic. Today, with the rise of strident nationalism in many East European nations and unemployment and economic insecurity throughout Europe, Roma continue to face widespread public prejudice and official discrimination.

THE HOLOCAUST:
The Destruction of European Jewry

THE NAZIS RESERVED THEIR MOST VICIOUS HATRED AND SYSTEMATIC GENOCIDAL plans for the Jews. Indeed, many of the measures they carried out against other groups—the imprisonment of political opponents or social nonconformers; the sterilization and murder of those with mental and physical disabilities; and the arrest, imprisonment, deportation, and murder of other so-called racial enemies—set the economic and social conditions; prepared the psychological ground; and offered the national security, military, and practical precedent for the mass killing of the Jews. The Nazis devoted themselves to this task as a priority and with a determination unmatched in the historical record. The success of their actions resulted in the almost complete annihilation of Jewish life and culture in Europe.

Nazi antisemitism grew out of a centuries-old tradition of hatred and fear of Jews as a religious, social, and cultural minority in Europe. Although Christianity began as a Jewish sect, Christians believed that Jesus of Nazareth was the Messiah and his arrival was the fulfillment of God's covenant with the people of Israel and of the Hebrew scriptures. Convinced that their religion superseded and replaced the Judaic faith, devout Christians further believed that the Jewish people were destined to wander the earth until they converted to Christianity. Jews were also vilified as "Christ-killers" and were blamed for the crucifixion.

In 70 C.E., Jews living in the province of Judea (now Israel) in the Roman Empire revolted against oppressive measures and were crushed by the legions of the Emperor Titus. His soldiers sacked the city of Jerusalem, destroyed the Temple, and banished the Jews from their holy land to the far reaches of Europe and Asia, scattering them from present-day Portugal to present-day Iran. They joined other Jews in exile, also known as the Diaspora, living among majority populations who did not share their beliefs and who often viewed them with suspicion and mistrust.

In 380 C.E., Christianity became the official state religion of the Roman Empire. In the centuries that followed, the Church was a powerful institution, aligned throughout Europe with the governing authorities. Jews were forced to the margins of society and banished to the role of perennial outsider. Most of the social, economic, and political restrictions against Jews had the explicit sanction of church leaders. Seminal Christian thinkers from Augustine in the fifth century to Martin Luther in the sixteenth denounced the Jews even as they sought to convert them. Increasingly, European culture understood itself as explicitly "Christian," and Jews were characterized as alien, inferior, disloyal, exploitative.

The status of Jews in western Europe remained tenuous until the modern era. With the English civil war in the seventeenth century and the French Revolution in 1789, Britain and France formed the vanguard of the emancipation movement, which gave civil and legal equality to Jews as religious kingdoms gave way to the modern national state.

By the late nineteenth century, Jews throughout western and central Europe had gained the same rights. Austria-Hungary granted equal rights to Jews in 1867; the newly united German Empire followed suit in 1871. Nevertheless, emancipation did not completely eliminate social discrimination and antisemitism. For generations, Europeans had feared and mistrusted Jews, seeing them as fundamentally foreign, untrustworthy, and inferior. Emancipation could not change the public perception overnight. At the same time, the legal foundation of equality allowed Jews to gradually assimilate into the larger cultural mainstream and to compete with Christians for job opportunities and careers, particularly in middle-class professions. Although antisemitism remained present throughout European societies and although members of all social groups held anti-Jewish opinions, Jews, nevertheless, were gaining status and security as the nineteenth century ended.

In contrast, most East European Jews, which before 1914 included the Jews of Russia, Romania, and the eastern borderlands of the German Empire and the Austro-Hungarian monarchy, lived in small, tightly knit communities called *shtetls*. They were separated from their Christian neighbors by virtue of faith, culture, and language. They maintained traditional religious observances and spoke in a German dialect called Yiddish. Although they, too, were granted equal citizenship rights in the aftermath of World War I, most Jews in Poland, Romania, Russia, and elsewhere still faced poverty, severe discrimination in the public and private sectors, and periodic outbreaks of mass violence known as *pogroms*. At the same time, in both East and West Europe, Jewish religious life, tradition, and culture remained rich and vibrant. Jewish artists, writers, scholars, and scientists thrived and made significant contributions to their fields of endeavor.

HERBERT MOSHEIM (second from the left) poses in costume with friends during *Karneval* (also known as *Fasching* or *Fastnacht*), which, like Mardi Gras, is a time of wild celebration, costume balls, and revelry leading up to the beginning of Lent. German Jews participated fully in the country's public life, and it was not unusual for assimilated Jewish families to take part in Christian holidays such as Karneval and Christmas. GERMANY, 1929–32. USHMM, COURTESY OF SUSAN MOSHEIM ALTERMAN

In 1933, the approximately 530,000 Jews in Germany constituted less than 1 percent of the total population of 67 million people. This relatively small minority was generally integrated in society; they tended to be proud of their citizenship in a country that had produced many great poets, writers, musicians, and artists. About 100,000 German Jews—a high percentage given their numbers—served in the German armed forces in World War I. Between 30,000 and 35,000 were decorated for bravery; some 12,000 died fighting. German Jews served in high public office; taught in universities; and were active in the arts, the sciences, the professions, and commerce. Of the 38 Nobel Prizes won by German writers and scientists between 1905 and 1936, 14 were awarded to Jews. During the first third of the twentieth century, intermarriage had become more common; often, Jews in such relationships converted to Christianity and raised their children in their new faith. Although some German Jews continued to encounter discrimination in their social lives and professional careers, many remained confident of their future under Weimar democracy. They spoke the German language and regarded the country as their home. Their identities as Germans seemed secure.

That confidence was badly shaken by the rise of the Nazi party and the appointment of Hitler as chancellor of Germany. Little more than a radical fringe element just five years earlier, Hitler and the Nazis were the largest and most powerful political party in the German parliament by 1933. From this newly won position of strength, many radicals within the Nazi movement were impatient to enact their long-standing agenda. Within the framework of Nazi ideology, nothing was more central than antisemitism—it served as impetus, rationale, and justification for virtually every major element of the party platform. Once in power, Hitler encouraged latent currents of anti-Jewish feeling in Germany and built upon those currents and other fears and prejudices to create and implement policies of exclusion, isolation, and eventually murder.

The nature of Nazi antisemitism is difficult to grapple with, in part because it was at one and the same time an outgrowth of the historical past and a relatively new formulation that diverged significantly from traditional manifestations of antisemitism. Historian Raul Hilberg proposed a framework that places the Nazis' beliefs and actions in the context of the whole history of Christian-based and secular antisemitism. He presents three successive trends: first, the Church attempted to convert Jews to Christianity; second, when mass conversion proved impossible and unsuccessful, the Church and then the secular leaders that followed it set out to banish the Jews from their midst by excluding them, segregating them, and forcing them into exile; third, when this effort failed to solve the so-called Jewish problem, the Nazis resolved to kill them. As Hilberg put it:

Since the fourth century after Christ, there have been three anti-Jewish policies: conversion, expulsion, and annihilation. The second appeared as an alternative to the first, and the third emerged as an alternative to the second. [...] The missionaries of Christianity had said in effect: You have no right to live among us as Jews. The secular rulers who followed had proclaimed: You have no right to live among us. The Nazis at last decreed: You have no right to live.

ANTISEMITIC POLICIES IN NAZI GERMANY, 1933–39

The Nazis did not take long to translate their antisemitic ideology into action. Over the course of the first 60 days of the Nazi regime, radicals within the party and its para-military organization, the SA (*Sturmabteilungen*), commonly known as storm troopers, attacked those who "looked Jewish." When reports of the street violence reached Great Britain and the United States, pressure mounted for an embargo of German-made goods, though no action was taken. In response, Hitler then ordered a boycott of Jewish-owned businesses in Germany. Calling the images of Jews being humiliated by Nazi storm troopers "atrocity propaganda," Hitler framed the boycott as a protest against Jewish efforts to tarnish the reputation of Germany abroad.

The boycott was the first public, nationwide move against the German Jewish community organized by the Nazi party. It began on the morning of Saturday April 1, 1933, as party radicals, storm troopers, and SS (*Schutzstaffel*), the elite guard of the Nazi party, paraded down the streets, warning the population not to shop in stores owned by Jews, and then blocked entrances to thousands of Jewish-owned businesses across the country. They painted Stars of David in yellow and black across doors and windows and carried signs emblazoned with antisemitic slogans.

Popular reaction was mixed. In many places, spontaneous violence erupted against Jews. Some Germans, however, made it a point of honor to enter Jewish-owned shops or to call on Jewish friends. Others complained that the Nazi rowdies disrupted their lives and contributed to public disorder. Many people continued to shop in their favorite stores regardless of the boycott. Reactions in the press outside Germany were almost universally disapproving.

Despite the mixed results, the Nazis predictably proclaimed the boycott a success. Less than a week later, Hitler issued the Law for the Restoration of the Professional Civil Service, which required, with a few exceptions, compulsory dismissal of Jews and other "non-Aryans" and of alleged political opponents of the nation from all government positions. This step

marked the beginning of a pattern that would repeat itself in years to come: anti-Jewish agitation from party activists, sanctioned by Hitler and the Nazi leadership, would consistently prompt the state bureaucracy to develop and implement discriminatory legislation against Jews and to prepare the German population to accept those "legal" measures. At the same time, because of the ambivalent response on the part of German citizenry to the April boycott, Hitler refrained from issuing further public policy statements about Jews. Over the next two years, Nazi anti-Jewish policy was generally characterized by the imposition of quotas in higher education; exclusion of Jews from state employment, the professions, and social organizations; and preferential treatment for non-Jews in a broad range of areas.

HANNE HIRSCH LIEBMANN (left) was born to a Jewish family in the German city of Karlsruhe in November 1924. Her father, Max, was a photographer. When he died in 1925, Hanne's mother, Ella, continued to maintain his studio. In 1930, Hanne began public school. Three years later, she experienced the boycott against Jewish businesses in Germany and the rising wave of antisemitism in her native country.

In April 1933, our studio, like the other Jewish businesses in Karlsruhe, was plastered with signs during the anti-Jewish boycott: "Don't buy from Jews." At school, a classmate made me so furious with her taunts that I ripped her sweater. After the November 1938 pogroms, the studio was busy making photos for the new ID cards marked "J" that Jews had to carry. The studio remained open until December 31 when all Jewish businesses had to be closed.

In 1940, Hanne was deported to the French-run detention camp of Gurs. Under the auspices of the Children's Aid Society, she eventually was sheltered in the French village of Le Chambon-sur-Lignon. After 1942, when roundups in France intensified, she was taken in by two different farming families. In early 1943, she escaped to Switzerland. Immediately after the war ended, she married Max Liebmann, and three years later she emigrated with her husband and daughter to the United States. LE CHAMBON, FRANCE, OCTOBER 18, 1942. USHMM, COURTESY OF JACK LEWIN

The 1933 pattern was repeated in 1935. After a spring and summer marred by both spontaneous and organized street violence against Jews throughout Germany, Hitler decreed and the Reich parliament enacted two laws on September 15, 1935, at the annual Nazi party rally in the city of Nuremberg. The Reich Citizenship Law and the Law for the Protection of German Blood and Honor would become the centerpiece of anti-Jewish legislation in Germany. Generally known as the Nuremberg Laws, the decrees defined who was and was not a Jew, and thus it clearly delineated between those who were encircled in the protective shelter of the state and those who were outside it. Under the Reich Citizenship Law, only people of "German or kindred blood" could claim the status of Reich citizen. German Jews were relegated to "subjects of the state" overnight.

The Law for the Protection of German Blood and Honor went on to legalize the segregation of Jewish and non-Jewish Germans by banning intermarriage and redefining sexual relations between them as "racial defilement," a crime that could be prosecuted. It also forbade German Jews to employ female non-Jewish household servants under the age of 45.

Throughout the centuries of antisemitic persecution in Europe, never before had a need to legally define Jewishness existed. Jews were guided in their behavior and customs by the principles of religious law and by generations of tradition. Those elements shaped virtually every aspect of daily life, including the clothing Jews wore, the language they spoke, the food they ate, and the holidays they celebrated. For hundreds of years, in concrete ways, and for better or worse, Jews were different and largely recognizable. By the time the Nazis took power, things had changed in Germany and elsewhere in Europe. No longer obvious outsiders, many Jews had given up the traditional ways and had adopted the cultural norms of mainstream society. Many abandoned the practice of Judaism and celebrated secular and Christian holidays, especially Christmas. In this context, identifying a Jew was not always easy. In the culture of fear and suspicion that the Nazis cultivated, they persuaded the German people that nothing was more important than knowing one's enemies. The Jews among them had to be identifiable once again.

Defining Jewishness was not easy. The Nazis rejected the long-standing view of Jews as members of a religious group and a cultural community. Instead, in keeping with their ideology of racial struggle, they insisted that Jewishness was conferred by birth and defined by blood descent. In their efforts to impose this new framework, however, the Nazis faced a problem. In spite of elaborate efforts to prove a biological essence of Jewishness using the pseudo-science of race hygiene, scientists could find no physical distinction between Jews and Germans. The Nazis, determined to define Jews as a race, sought to find their way around the problem by looking to familial ancestry, rather than personal religious observance or belief, as the solution.

Under the Nuremberg Laws, people with three or more grandparents born into the Jewish religious community counted as Jews in Nazi Germany. Although the Nazis called this a "racial" definition for propagandistic reasons, they depended, in fact, on membership in the Jewish community—rather than blood type, physical characteristics, or other so-called racial identifiers—as the source of a person's origins. The starting point for Jewish identity was establishing religious affiliation—two generations back—and then defining those people's grandparents as "racially" Jewish. Furthermore, the general principle led to elaborate variations, including certain exceptions and definitions of those who were "part-Jewish" (*Mischlinge*). Despite the persistent rhetoric of Nazi ideology, no scientifically valid basis existed for designating Jews as a race.

The Nazis' action had the net effect of imposing a Jewish identity on tens of thousands of people who did not think of themselves as Jews or who had no religious and cultural ties to that community. Furthermore, the law classified as Jews many who had converted from Judaism or even whose parents or grandparents had adopted another religion. Thus, practicing Roman Catholics and Protestants—even priests, ministers, and nuns—suddenly found themselves defined as Jews and, just as abruptly, stripped of their citizenship and deprived of their basic rights.

The Nuremberg Laws, in effect, reversed emancipation and unraveled the gains that Jews had made in Germany over the previous century. Still worse, they laid the foundation for future antisemitic measures by unequivocally dividing the nation into "Aryan" Germans and Jews. For the first time in history, Jews were oppressed not for what they believed, but for who they—or their parents—were by birth. As a result, the terms of the law made Jewish identity impossible to deny or alter, representing a fundamental break with the antisemitism of the past. In Nazi Germany, no profession of belief, no change of affinity, and no act or statement on the part of a Jew could release him or her from the destiny decreed by the state.

In Nazi Germany, propaganda was the face and voice of the Nazi party, constantly reminding the German people how they must think and act. In March 1933, shortly after the Nazis seized power, Hitler had established a Reich Ministry of Public Enlightenment and Propaganda headed by Joseph Goebbels. Its aim was to ensure that the Nazi message was successfully communicated through the news media (radio and print journalism) and educational material, as well as through art, music, theater, films, books, and other forms of entertaiment. Hitler described the function of propaganda in *Mein Kampf,* when he advocated its use to spread the Nazi ideals of racism, antisemitism, and anti-Bolshevism. "Propaganda attempts to force a doctrine on the whole people," he wrote; "propaganda works on the general public from the standpoint of an idea and makes them ripe for the victory of this idea."

Propaganda addressed all aspects of daily life. Within this overwhelming barrage of political, social, and cultural pressure, the Nazis orchestrated an antisemitic propaganda campaign designed to cultivate fear and hatred of Jews. Nazi propaganda attempted to convince ordinary Germans that Jews were an alien people, who were separate from and hostile to the nation and to the German "Aryan" race. Images depicted Jews as grotesque caricatures and presented them as scheming, cunning profiteers who fed off Germany for their own ends. Jews were portrayed as the antithesis of the pure "Aryan" German, who was tall, muscular, and fair, with finely chiseled features, and who was usually shown working at physical labor in the service of the nation. Propaganda artists established a visual vocabulary that worked on the German collective psyche, thus linking the image of "Aryans" with the beautiful, the good, and the noble and, conversely, associating Jews with ugliness, dishonesty, greed, and destructiveness. This two-pronged approach—the glorification of the Nazi regime, its leaders, and its goals, on one hand, and the intense vilification of its so-called enemies, on the other—left no room for ambiguity in the public imagination. Above all, anti-Jewish propaganda sent a message to Germans that the Jews were an enemy lying in wait, plotting to harm the Fatherland. Every aspect of Nazi anti-semitic propaganda was coordinated to ensure that Germans would fear and despise the Jews and would eventually accept legal measures against them.

Another way in which the Nazis secured public acceptance of antisemitic policy was by gradually, incrementally, and unrelentingly implementing anti-Jewish legislation. During the first six years of Hitler's dictatorship, from 1933 until the outbreak of war in 1939, Jews felt the effects of more than 400 decrees and regulations that restricted all aspects of their public and private lives. Many of those laws were national ones that had been issued by the German administration and affected all Jews. But state, regional, and municipal officials, on their own initiative, also promulgated a barrage of exclusionary decrees against Jews in their own communities. Thus, hundreds of individuals in all levels of government throughout the country were involved in the persecution of Jews as they conceived, discussed, drafted, adopted, enforced, and supported anti-Jewish legislation. No corner of Germany was left untouched.

The first wave of legislation, from 1933 to 1934, focused largely on limiting the participation of Jews in German public life. As described previously, the April 1933 Law for the Restoration of the Professional Civil Service forced half of the approximately 5,000 Jewish government employees out of their jobs. During the same year, the city of Berlin forbade Jewish lawyers and notaries to work on legal matters, the mayor of Munich disallowed Jewish doctors from treating non-Jewish patients, and the Bavarian Interior Ministry denied admission of Jewish students to medical school. At the national level, the Nazi government revoked the licenses of Jewish tax consultants; imposed a 1.5 percent quota on admission of "non-Aryans" to public schools and universities; fired Jewish civilian workers from the army; and, in early 1934, forbade Jewish actors to perform on the stage or screen. Local governments also issued regulations that affected other spheres of Jewish life: in Saxony, Jews could no longer slaughter animals according to ritual purity requirements, effectively preventing them from obeying the Jewish dietary laws.

The Nuremberg Laws of 1935 heralded a new wave of antisemitic legislation that brought about immediate and concrete segregation: Jewish patients were no longer admitted to municipal hospitals in Dusseldorf, German court judges could not cite legal commentaries or opinions written by Jewish authors, Jewish officers were expelled from the army, and Jewish university students were not allowed to sit for doctoral exams. Other regulations reinforced the message that Jews were outsiders in Germany; for example, in December 1935, the Reich Propaganda Ministry issued a decree forbidding Jewish soldiers to be named among the dead in World War I memorials.

Government agencies at all levels aimed to exclude Jews from the economic sphere of Germany by preventing them from earning a living. Jews were required to register their domestic and foreign property and assets, a prelude to the gradual expropriation of their material wealth by the state. Likewise, the German authorities intended to "Aryanize" all Jewish businesses, a process involving the dismissal of Jewish workers and managers, as well as the transfer of companies and enterprises to non-Jewish Germans, who bought them at prices officially fixed well below market value. From April 1933 to April 1938, "Aryanization" effectively reduced the number of Jewish-owned businesses in Germany by approximately two-thirds.

By 1938, the signs grew still more foreboding as the government required Jews to identify themselves in ways that would permanently separate them from the rest of the population. In January, they were prohibited by law from changing their personal names and the following April from altering the names of their businesses. Then, in August, Jews whose names were not considered ethnically identifiable were required to adopt the middle name Israel (for men) and Sara (for women). Finally, in October, Jews were required to revalidate their passports, a procedure that involved marking the document with a large red J.

This legislative assault had a powerful psychological component, which not only worked against the Jews but also implicated the German citizenry. The government issued laws gradually over a span of many years, and this incremental quality served to camouflage the escalation that was, in fact, taking place. In that way, much of the non-Jewish German public—as well as many Jews—were lulled into a false sense of complacency, thus accommodating and normalizing each individual step. For the Nazis, however, each law facilitated still more restrictive measures that weakened and demoralized individual

Jews and the community as a whole while increasing the divide between Jews and non-Jews. Moreover, the economic benefits that many non-Jewish Germans drew from the consequences of this legislation reinforced their personal stake and interest in the survival of the Nazi regime.

Until Nazi Germany started World War II in 1939, antisemitic legislation in Germany served to "encourage" and ultimately to force a mass emigration of German Jews. The Nazi government did all it could to induce the Jews to leave Germany. In addition to making life miserable, the German authorities reduced bureaucratic hurdles so those who wanted to leave could do so more easily. At the same time, the Nazis viewed the Jews' belongings and their financial capital as German property, and they had no intention of allowing refugees to take anything of material value with them. Most of those who fled had to relinquish title to homes and businesses, and were subject to increasingly heavy emigration taxes that reduced their assets. Furthermore, the German authorities restricted how much money could be transferred abroad from German banks, and they allowed each passenger to take only ten reichsmarks (about U.S. $4) out of the country. Most German Jews who managed to emigrate were completely impoverished by the time they were able to leave.

A refugee girl (left) arrives in Harwich, Great Britain, as part of a *Kindertransport* (Children's Transport) on December 2, 1938. For humanitarian reasons, Great Britain allowed the immigration of approximately 10,000 unaccompanied Jewish children from Nazi Germany. A similar provision providing a haven for Jewish children fleeing Nazi Germany, the Wagner-Rogers Act, failed in Congress in the United States. HARWICH, GREAT BRITAIN, DECEMBER 2, 1938. USHMM, COURTESY OF STADTMUSEUM BADEN-BADEN

Many nations in which the German Jews sought asylum imposed significant obstacles to immigration. Application processes for entry visas were elaborate and demanding,

Most German Jews who managed to emigrate

were completely impoverished

by the time they were able to leave.

requiring prospective immigrants to provide information about themselves and their family members from banks, doctors, and the German police. In the case of the United States, applicants were required to provide affidavits from multiple sponsors and to have secured a waiting number within a quota established for their country of birth, which severely limited their chances to emigrate. All this red tape existed against the backdrop of other hardships: competition with thousands of equally desperate people, slow mail that made communication with would-be sponsors difficult, financial hardships, and oppressive measures in Germany that made even the simplest task a chore. Finally, many who wanted to flee had, by necessity, to apply to numerous countries for entry. It is no wonder that for many Jews in Germany in the 1930s, the attempt to emigrate was more than a full-time job.

The years in the late 1930s were particularly ill-suited for a major refugee crisis. A severe worldwide economic depression reinforced through Europe and the United States an existing fear and mistrust of foreigners in general, as well as antisemitism in particular. Above all, people were wary of immigrants who might compete for their jobs, burden their already beleaguered social services, or be tempted as impoverished workers by the promises of labor agitators or domestic Communist movements. Even government officials in democratic countries were not immune to those sentiments. Most foreign countries, including the United States, Canada, and Great Britain, were unwilling to increase their immigrant quotas to admit very large groups of refugees, especially the impoverished and the dispossessed. Indeed, the United States refused to reduce the myriad obstacles to getting an immigrant visa, with the result that until 1938, the immigration quota for Germany was unfilled. Many German Jews who were in immediate danger were forced to emigrate elsewhere, such as France, Holland, and Czechoslovakia, where eventually the wave of German conquest overtook them.

The bureaucratic hurdles for emigration were overwhelming. Far from streamlining the process to allow more refugees to enter, nations required extensive documentation that was often virtually impossible to obtain. In some cases, refugees literally faced a "catch-22": proof of passage booked on a ship was required for a visa, and proof of a visa was required to book passage on a ship.

The following is a list of the documents required by the United States to obtain a visa:
· Five copies of the visa application
· Two copies of applicant's birth certificate
· Quota number (establishing the applicant's place on the waiting list)
· Two sponsors:

- Close relatives of the prospective immigrant were preferred
- The sponsors were required to be U.S. citizens or to have permanent resident status, and they were required to have completed and notarized six copies of an Affidavit of Support and Sponsorship

· Supporting documents:
- Certified copy of most recent federal tax return
- Affidavit from a bank regarding applicant's accounts
- Affidavit from any other responsible person regarding other assets, (affidavit from sponsor's employer or statement of commercial rating)

· Certificate of Good Conduct from German Police authorities, including two copies of each:
- Police dossier
- Prison record
- Military record
- Other government records about individual

· Affidavits of Good Conduct (after September 1940) from several responsible disinterested persons

· Physical examination at U.S. consulate

· Proof of permission to leave Germany (imposed September 30, 1939)

· Proof that prospective immigrant had booked passage to the Western hemisphere (imposed September 1939)

After Germany annexed Austria in March 1938 and Nazi-sponsored street violence in both Austria and Germany dramatically increased the numbers of German and Austrian Jews seeking to emigrate, pressure mounted on U.S. President Franklin D. Roosevelt to address the intensified refugee crisis. He responded by proposing an international conference to be held in the French resort town of Evian-les-Bains on July 6–15, 1938. At the same time, the tenor of the invitation was indicative of U.S. and international ambivalence about the refugee situation. Thirty-three nations were invited with the reassurance that "no country will be expected... to receive a greater number of immigrants than is permitted by existing legislation." The invitation further pointed out that refugee assistance programs would be financed by private agencies and emphasized that no government funds would be required. In addition, Great Britain was assured that the subject of Jewish immigration into Palestine would not be discussed. President Roosevelt did not send his secretary of state to the conference; instead, he dispatched Myron C. Taylor, a businessman and his personal friend, to represent the United States.

Two days after Roosevelt announced the Evian Conference, Adolf Hitler remarked, "I can only hope that the other world, which has such deep sympathy for these criminals [the Jews], will at least be generous enough to convert this sympathy into practical aid. We on our part are ready to put all these criminals at the disposal of these countries—for all I care, even on luxury ships."

The delegations from the invited nations did not convert sympathy into practical aid. Representatives from country after country stood up and acknowledged the refugees' plight but offered excuses and justifications for refusing to open their doors. Great Britain would admit few Jews and kept Palestine closed to large-scale Jewish immigration. Canada was willing to accept farmers, but this opportunity did not help the urban-dwelling Jews of Austria and Germany. Australia declined to assist because, in the words of its representative, it "does not have a racial problem, and [is] not desirous of importing one." For its part, the United States continued to refuse to increase the number of immigrants it would allow or to reduce the overwhelming bureaucratic hurdles involved in obtaining a visa. Only the Dominican Republic offered substantial aid by agreeing to allow 100,000 Jews to enter its tiny country.

The consequences of the Evian Conference were dire for the Jews of Germany. They were no better off in practical terms than they had been before the conference, yet their oppressors seemed vindicated by the reluctance of Europe and the Americas to help them. Adolf Hitler, himself, addressed the matter at the Party Congress in Nuremberg on September 12, 1938: "They complain ... of the boundless cruelty with which Germany—and now Italy also—seek to rid themselves of their Jewish elements.... But lamentations have not led these democratic countries to substitute helpful activity.... [O]n the contrary, these countries with icy coldness assured us that obviously there was no place for the Jews in their territory...." Although Hitler's government would not implement the murder of the European Jewish population for three more years, the events of Evian provided Nazi leaders with a useful propaganda tool to explain why emigration would not work and to justify more extreme measures of "removing" the Jews from German "living spaces."

On November 7, 1938, a Polish Jewish student living in Paris was angered at Germany's treatment of his parents, Polish Jews who had been living and working in Germany but who had been expelled recently. He assassinated a German diplomat at the embassy in Paris. The Nazi leadership seized the opportunity to portray the act as an organized effort by their enemies to destroy Germany. Just as they had blamed the Communists for the Reichstag fire in 1933 and used the event to step up violence against their political enemies, the Nazis accused "world Jewry" of orchestrating the assassination. In reprisal, they unleashed a massive pogrom throughout the Reich, which by then included Austria and the Sudeten German regions of Czechoslovakia. Although the Nazis presented the events that followed as a spontaneous outburst of public rage, the pogrom was, in fact, instigated and carried out by Nazi party officials, storm troopers, SS men, and Hitler Youth. Its purpose was to prepare the German people to accept and endorse a new wave of legislation aimed at eliminating the Jews entirely from the economic life of Germany and forcing their expulsion from Germany.

The violence began on November 9 and lasted through November 10, 1938, with sporadic acts of violence over the following days. The Nazis destroyed more than 250 synagogues, including many of the finest Jewish houses of worship in all of Europe, and they damaged beyond repair thousands of precious ritual objects. They attacked anything that was associated with Jews, thereby desecrating cemeteries; vandalizing businesses and homes; looting property; and, in many cases, assaulting and even killing individuals. At least 91 Jews were killed during the pogrom. Some ordinary citizens joined in the destruction of property and physical assault on people, while others looked on, appalled by the violence and disorder.

On orders from Gestapo headquarters, the German police rounded up about 30,000 Jewish men and incarcerated most of them in concentration camps. There the SS guards treated them brutally; hundreds died within days or weeks of their arrival. The pogrom is known as "The Night of Broken Glass" (*Kristallnacht*) to describe the wanton destruction of glass windows that littered the streets of German cities after the authorities finally put an end to the violence.

To add insult to injury, the Nazis blamed Jews for provoking the attack and held them financially responsible for the cleanup. The Nazis imposed on the victims a penalty of one billion reichsmarks (the equivalent of US$400 million at 1938 rates) and made Jews liable for the repair of their damaged homes, shops, and synagogues. As a further burden, the government appropriated the insurance payments owed to Jewish clients. Store and home-owners were made to repair their buildings and replace their property at their own expense.

"The Night of Broken Glass" marked a turning point and prepared the political and psychological atmosphere for yet another wave of anti-Jewish legislation. In the weeks that followed, the government issued dozens of laws and decrees that deprived Jews of their property and prevented them from earning a livelihood. The regulations also excluded Jews from all aspects of public social life: the German authorities barred them from all public schools and universities, as well as cinemas, theaters, and sports facilities. In many cities, Jews were forbidden to enter designated "Aryan" zones, to enter public parks, and to sit on certain benches. By the end of 1938, the driver's licenses of Jews had been revoked, and all their financial assets were frozen.

Meanwhile, Nazi aims regarding Jewish emigration escalated from encouragement to outright force. Of the tens of thousands of Jewish men who had been arrested and sent

to concentration camps, most were released only after they proved that they had made arrangements to emigrate from Germany and to transfer their property and assets to non-Jews. Under unprecedented pressure by their own government, tens of thousands of Jews lined up at foreign consulates seeking visas and immigration papers.

The Jewish synagogue in Baden-Baden, Germany (left), continues to burn the morning after "The Night of Broken Glass," November 9–10, 1938. Synagogues occupy a central place in Jewish religious and communal life. To the Nazis, however, they served as a powerful physical reminder of the presence of Jews in Germany. The Nazis destroyed 250 synagogues in German-occupied territory during "The Night of Broken Glass." BADEN-BADEN, GERMANY, NOVEMBER 10, 1938. USHMM, COURTESY OF STADTMUSEUM BADEN-BADEN

Still, the international community failed to sufficiently loosen requirements, increase quotas, and streamline bureaucratic processes. In 1939, the United States finally—and for the first time—filled its combined German-Austrian quota (which, after March 1939 included the incorporated Czech provinces of Bohemia and Moravia). However, that limit did not come close to meeting the demand. By the end of June 1939, 309,000 German, Austrian, and Czech Jews had applied for only 27,000 places available under the U.S. quota. Ultimately, only 43,450 Jews from Germany, Austria, and the Czech lands immigrated to the United States in 1939. Other efforts by Americans to help the beleaguered Jews of Germany failed. In particular, the Wagner-Rogers Bill, an effort to admit 20,000 endangered Jewish refugee children on an emergency basis, failed to pass the U.S. Senate in 1939 and again in 1940.

The administrative obstacles to emigration were the most concrete, but not always the most pressing, reason that people failed to exit Germany in time. German Jews thought of themselves as Germans, and many simply could not accept that the rights and privileges that had been theirs since emancipation had been so completely swept away. Until "The

Night of Broken Glass," German Jews had been tempted to believe that Nazism was a temporary reactionary swing and that the most reasonable and prudent stance was to be patient, to endure, and to wait for it to blow over. In addition, many German Jews—especially those who were established, middle or upper class, and culturally assimilated—had much to lose. The thought of fleeing their homes, leaving behind family, friends, jobs and professions, community, and all other familiar elements of daily life was emotionally agonizing. Germany had been their home for generations, and their attachment to the country of their birth kept them from understanding and accepting the precariousness of their position. Indeed, to leave was to accept that they were no longer German citizens but Jewish refugees. For many, the full understanding and recognition of the danger they faced did not become clear until it was too late.

Despite the difficulties faced in trying to emigrate, by 1939, about half the German Jewish population and more than two-thirds of Austrian Jews had fled Nazi persecution. The ones who were able to emigrate settled mainly in Palestine, the United States, and Central and South America. Under a program known as the Children's Transport (*Kindertransport*), 10,000 unaccompanied Jewish children were admitted to Great Britain during 1938–39. More than 18,000 Jews from the German Reich were also able to find refuge in Shanghai, in Japanese-occupied China. Still others made their way into other European nations where they would be caught again in the Nazi net during the war.

WORLD WAR II

Nazi leaders planned World War II to accelerate the accomplishment of their long-term goals. First and foremost, they wanted to conquer "living space" (*Lebensraum*), so that the "Aryan" German race would have room to expand and thereby survive. Simultaneously, the conflict would provide a cover and a justification to physically eliminate "racial" enemies, especially the Jews, which the Nazis viewed as their highest priority. The Nazis drew on the domestic consensus, or at least acquiescence, that they had carefully built among the Germans to implement their territorial conquests.

As stated earlier, German forces invaded Poland on September 1, 1939. Two days later, Britain and France declared war on Germany; they had issued a guarantee of Poland's borders five months earlier in an attempt to force Germany to negotiate for territorial acquisition and to prevent military action. When their approach failed, the nations of Europe found themselves at war.

Using the heightened sense of national emergency that accompanied the outbreak of hostilities, the Nazi government imposed new decrees that discriminated against the Jews who remained in Germany. Authorities subjected the Jewish population to a strict curfew, excluded them from certain areas of cities, and limited the time periods in which they could purchase provisions and supplies. When food rationing began, the German authorities allotted reduced amounts for Jews and forbade them from buying certain items. German authorities also ordered Jews to turn in their radios, electrical appliances, bicycles, and cars to the police.

Additionally, the defeat and occupation of Poland by the German army in less than a month brought nearly two million Polish Jews under German authority. This development, as well as the refusal of Britain and France to accept Hitler's offer to negotiate peace, further complicated efforts to expel the Jews from areas in which Germans lived. Enemies of Germany closed their borders to immigration from Germany, virtually denying would-be emigrants a path to safety or a country willing to take them. The Nazi leadership had to deal with a vastly increased Jewish population and few ways to force them out of territory under German control.

Faced with such obstacles, the Nazis considered the idea of establishing a so-called Jewish reservation. It was a concept that had been put forth as a solution to the "Jewish question" in the nineteenth century and that regained currency among high-ranking Nazis in the late 1930s. Before the war, planners had speculated that such a place would be established by international action. In the face of the war, Nazi planners clearly saw that they would have to act unilaterally, locating the reservation on territory under German occupation.

When, in May 1940, the Germans invaded and swiftly conquered the western European countries of France, the Netherlands, Belgium, and Luxembourg, the Nazi leadership saw other possibilities open up for mass expulsion of the Jews to a given location. In particular, the German victory over France led some policy planners to turn their attention to the large French island colony of Madagascar off the east coast of Africa. They focused on the idea of establishing a Jewish reservation there, because it was far from lands on which Germans might settle. The concept of the Madagascar plan depended on a German victory over or accommodation with the British, the continued neutrality of the United States, and devotion of considerable naval and security resources to the removal of Jews. The uncertainty of peace with or victory over the British became clear within weeks of the armistice with France, and by September 1940, continued British domination of the seas was clear.

As Hitler's attention turned eastward toward the Soviet Union and a war that the Nazis had always planned to fight, interest in Madagascar began to wane. At the same time, Hitler's preparation for invading the Soviet Union brought core Nazi goals into sharp focus. A "final solution" to the "Jewish question" in Europe made sense only in the

context of the do-or-die struggle between German Nazism and Soviet communism. The Nazi leadership knew that the invasion of the Soviet Union would bring still more Jews under German control and that the principle of preemptive action to subdue the "Jewish-Bolshevik" enemy created an ideological and psychological atmosphere favoring even more-radical solutions.

The youngest of seven children, MOISHE FELMAN (left) was raised in a Yiddish-speaking, religious Jewish home in Sokolow Podlaski, in central Poland. Moishe's parents ran a grain business. Moishe attended a Jewish school and began public school in Sokolow Podlaski in 1933.

Summer vacation had just finished, and 13-year-old Moishe was about to begin another year at elementary school when the Germans invaded Poland on September 1, 1939. German aircraft bombed Sokolow Podlaski's market and other civilian targets before German troops entered the town on September 20. Three days later, they set fire to the main synagogue. Later, the Germans confiscated the family's grain business.

Over the next two years, the Germans imposed restrictions on the Jews, eventually ordering them to wear an identifying Star of David on their clothing. On September 28, 1941, the Germans set up a ghetto and concentrated all of the town's Jews there. About a year later, on the most solemn holiday of the Jewish religion, the Day of Atonement, the Germans began to round up the people in the ghetto. Those who resisted or tried to hide were shot. Moishe, his mother, and sister were herded onto the boxcar of a train.

On September 22, 1942, Moishe and his family were deported to the Treblinka extermination camp. He was gassed there shortly after arriving. He was 16 years old. NO DATE OR PLACE GIVEN. USHMM.

The Nazis saw the conundrum in increasingly stark terms: on the one hand, they endorsed an unshakable imperative to remove the Jews; on the other hand, they had increasingly limited options to fulfill that goal. Although scholars still debate the timing of the decision to physically annihilate the Jews of Europe, the steps the Nazi leadership would take against the Jews in the Soviet Union would shape and focus their thinking on that unprecedented and most radical "solution" to the dilemma of the "Jewish problem."

While the Nazi leadership deliberated about what to do with Europe's Jews, those leaders took the intermediate step of concentrating, containing, controlling, and isolating them in manageable pockets throughout Poland. The Nazis used as their model the medieval ghetto, an area of town designated by Church authorities as a place where Jews were permitted to reside but were kept strictly separate from the Christian population. In the twentieth century, ghettos in German-occupied eastern Europe were typically composed of a small number of streets surrounded by barbed wire, fences, or stone walls in the poorest part of a city or town. In more-rural areas, ghettos were often not enclosed at all and, in some cases, constituted the entire town. From the outset, the ghettos were conceived not as a permanent solution to the "Jewish question" but as a provisional measure to control, isolate, and segregate Jews pending their complete removal from territories under German control.

The ghettos established by the German authorities were located primarily in eastern Europe between 1940 and 1943 and in Hungary in 1944. Seeing no need to expend resources on Jewish inhabitants, German occupation policy ensured virtually unlivable conditions in most ghettos. They were severely overcrowded, little existed in the way of sanitation or other measures to control disease, they generally lacked heat and electricity, and food rations were almost always substandard and drastically limited. The brutal and primitive living conditions heavily increased mortality rates from epidemic disease, mass starvation, and exposure.

Jewish children (right) holding bowls for soup rations in the Warsaw ghetto in Poland, between 1940 and 1943. The deprivations of ghetto life affected children with particular severity, turning many of them into beggars and food smugglers. Weakened by hunger and disease, younger children in the ghetto died more quickly than adults did; infants were the first to perish. A small percentage of Jewish children were rescued by non-Jews, who hid them from the German authorities and their accomplices. WARSAW, POLAND, C.1940. USHMM, COURTESY OF INSTYTUT PAMIECI NARODOWEJ

The ghettos were conceived... as a provisional measure

to control, isolate, and segregate Jews

pending their complete removal

from territories under German control.

Initially created as a short-term measure, ghettos existed for as long as three years in occupied Poland (and later in the Soviet Union). During that time, German enterprises, including those owned by the armed forces, the SS, the civilian occupation authorities, and private individuals, took the opportunity to exploit the residents for inexpensive forced labor. Some Jewish ghetto administrations sought investment in the ghettos, particularly from the army and the private sector, in the hope of improving conditions and even ensuring survival in return for production of usable goods. The German civilian authorities continued to allot food and supply rations that were just enough to keep alive those able to work, while those who were weakened by exhaustion or illness inevitably died. Hard labor came to dominate the lives of ghetto inhabitants, and they quickly came to see a relationship between their ability to produce—individually and collectively—and their ongoing survival.

By 1941, conditions in the ghettos in German-occupied Poland had deteriorated to such an extent that they were places of mass death. The results could hardly have been otherwise, considering the Germans' deliberate neglect of the residents' basic needs. Some historians have argued that, had the Germans left the harsh ghetto regime intact, Polish Jewry might well have been annihilated within ten years. Although those ghettos in which both military and private entrepreneurs had invested significantly had advocates for continued existence among the German civilian administrators, the SS and police—who used ideological and security arguments—and German health officials in the occupation bureaucracy—who feared epidemics that might spread to the non-Jewish population—won the debate.

German *Einsatzgruppen* (Mobile Killing Squad) soldiers guard Jewish women and children (right) before massacring them. In the background, other Jews are forced to undress and their clothing is heaped on the ground. This photo, originally in color, was part of a series taken by a German military photographer. Copies from this collection were later used as evidence in war crimes trials. LUBNY, [UKRAINE] USSR, OCTOBER 16, 1941. WITH PERMISSION OF THE HAMBURGER INSTITUT FÜR SOZIALFORSCHUNG

The Nazis, and many other Germans understood the war

as a life-and-death struggle between two world views—

the "German/Aryan" and the "Jewish/communist"—

in which no compromise was possible.

Moreover, in the first months of 1941, the Nazi leaders were deep in planning for the invasion of the Soviet Union, which would, in turn, bring millions more Jews under their control. Against the backdrop of the failed plans for mass expulsion and plans to initiate the conflict that would destroy the archenemy of National Socialism, the Nazi leaders took a first, practical step toward the "Final Solution"; they planned the murder of the Jewish population throughout the Soviet Union.

Germany invaded the Soviet Union on June 22, 1941, violating the existing nonaggression pact between the two countries and initiating a war that would make genocide possible. The Germans presented the invasion as a historic struggle against the Bolshevik ideology, which was supposedly disseminated by Jews, and as an attack on the Soviet Union, which was the seat of world communism. More than other conflicts, the Nazis and many other Germans understood the war as a life-and-death struggle between two world views—the "German/Aryan" and the "Jewish/Communist"—in which no compromise was possible. In this context, German authorities gave their invading forces explicit orders to target for annihilation all potential enemies, particularly Jews, Roma, members of the Soviet state and Communist Party elites, and anyone else who might oppose their permanent rule.

Mobile Killing Squads of German SS and police personnel, who followed the German army as it advanced deep into Soviet territory, were tasked with identifying and murdering those whom they perceived to be racial or political enemies of Germany, as well as developing intelligence nets to flush out those enemies who were not immediately visible. Because Nazi ideology defined Soviet Jews as especially dangerous, the Mobile Killing Squads, together with the auxiliary forces that they recruited from local collaborators and the German Order Police units that reinforced them, first shot primarily Jewish men of arms-bearing age, then buried them in mass graves. By the end of July, however, German forces began to annihilate entire Jewish communities—men, women, and children—without regard for age or sex. Those who were able to flee the massacres were often killed by the local population or turned over to the Germans to be shot. SS and police units also killed Roma and officials of the Soviet state and the Communist Party, as well as thousands of residents of institutions for people with mental and physical disabilities.

The civilian German administrator of the Belorussian town of Slutsk witnessed and reported on a massacre in his locale as follows:

As far as the manner in which this action was carried out, it is with deepest regret that I have to state that this bordered on the sadistic.... The Jewish people but also [non-Jewish] White Russians were taken from their homes and rounded up with indescribable brutality by both the German police officials and, in particular, the Lithuanian partisans. Gunfire could be heard everywhere in the town and the bodies of the executed Jews piled up in the streets.... I was not present at the shooting which took place outside the town. I cannot, therefore, make any remarks about the brutality. It should however suffice to say that some time after the graves had been filled up victims managed to work their way out of them.

One of the most infamous massacre sites was Babi Yar, a ravine situated just outside Kiev in Ukraine. By the time the Germans captured Kiev on September 19, 1941, more than half the Jews who lived there had managed to flee. Ten days after taking the city, the Germans ordered the remaining Jews to report for supposed resettlement. Jews who ignored the German order faced the death penalty. Whole families, from infants to grandparents, followed the German directive and appeared at the assembly point, having no idea of the fate that awaited them. They were directed to proceed along Melnik Street toward the Jewish cemetery and into an area that included the cemetery itself and a part of the Babi Yar ravine. It was cordoned off by a barbed-wire fence and guarded by Germans and Ukrainian auxiliary police. As the Jews approached the ravine, they were forced to hand over their valuables, take off all their clothes, and advance toward the ravine edge in groups of ten. When they reached the edge, German SS and police gunned them down with automatic weapons. At the end of the day, the bodies were covered over with a thin layer of soil. In two days of shooting, the Germans and their auxiliaries had killed more than 33,000 Jews. In the months that followed, thousands more were killed at Babi Yar, including many Roma and Soviet prisoners of war. The final death toll at Babi Yar has been estimated at 100,000.

Most men of the Mobile Killing Squads were ideologically committed individuals, but they drew support and reinforcement from tens of thousands of German Order Police and military personnel, many of whom had not joined either the Nazi party or the SS. The killing units also depended on assistance from local populations, who were not necessarily adherents of Nazi ideology but whose actions clearly represented a willingness to kill Jews and Communists. Many scholars believe that the systematic slaughter of Jews in the occupied Soviet Union was a critical test of the readiness of ordinary people—both German and non-German—to acquiesce and in some cases to participate in organized mass murder.

THE "FINAL SOLUTION"

The "Final Solution" was the Nazis' comprehensive program to solve the "Jewish question" by murdering every Jew in Europe. It was the culmination of a process in Nazi anti-Jewish

policy that began with legal discrimination against Jews in Germany, transitioned to coercive emigration and schemes for mass expulsion, and then escalated from the mass murder of the Soviet Jews to the attempted annihilation of the entire Jewish population of Europe.

A family (left) poses for a photograph in the prewar Polish town known in Yiddish as Eishishok and in Polish as Ejszyszki (present-day Eišiškes, Lithuania). The history of this town mirrors that of many Jewish communities in eastern Europe. German troops arrived on June 23, 1941, and less than three months later, on September 21, an SS Mobile Killing Squad entered the town, accompanied by Lithuanian auxiliaries. Four thousand Jews from Eishishok and its environs were herded into three synagogues and imprisoned there. They were taken in groups of 250 to the old Jewish cemetery where SS men ordered them to undress and stand at the edge of open pits. There, Lithuanian auxiliary troops shot them to death. Over only a few days, the massacre ended 900 years of Jewish life and culture in Eishishok. Today, no Jews live there. EISHISHOK (PRESENT-DAY EIŠIŠKES, LITHUANIA), BEFORE 1941. WITH PERMISSION OF THE SHTETL FOUNDATION

The exact timing of the decision to implement the "Final Solution" will probably never be known and remains a subject of debate among scholars. Implementation of the policy surely was accelerated by the unparalleled success of German forces in the Soviet Union in the summer of 1941, when the prospect of victory over the Soviets and indeed all of Europe seemed within reach. After the SS and police had begun to physically annihilate entire Jewish communities in the east, mass murder became not only conceivable but also achievable in practice—a more "final" solution than mass expulsion. But some of the inherent problems in the killing operations in the Soviet Union rendered them difficult, if not impossible, to implement elsewhere in German-occupied Europe. Murder by shooting in open-air pits was slow, inefficient, and psychologically traumatic for some of the shooters; also, it tended in the long term to awaken genuine unrest in the indigenous populations.

The tactics used by the German authorities to kill Jews in Russia could not be exported to Germany and western Europe. Outright killings in plain sight of the local populations not only would present serious opposition to the Nazi regime, but also would allow news of the atrocities to spread throughout the world at large. Mindful of those issues, the SS and police leaders merged elements of their past programs to develop the "Final Solution." In addition to continuing the police shootings in the Soviet Union and the General Government, the SS and police leaders established stationary killing centers at locations convenient to deportation of the large numbers of Polish Jews. Using the model of the "euthanasia" program gas chambers or the gas vans that had been used in Serbia and Soviet Russia, they chose as a killing method suffocation with carbon monoxide or Zyklon B gas. To ensure security and to facilitate deception, the Nazis located the killing centers in areas of Poland that were distant from the German and west European population centers; they were also at some distance from the major ghettos where the Polish Jews were concentrated. To guarantee both security and secrecy, the Germans would carry out the actual gassing operations inside secured enclosures, surrounded by barbed wire and guarded on the perimeter. Drawing on the experience of earlier population resettlement programs, the Germans would transport the Jews to their deaths using existing European rail routes, augmented by special rail spurs into the killing centers themselves. The German authorities planned to hide the murders behind the deceptive facade of "Resettlement in the East." In the autumn of 1941, SS and police officials began the construction of special gassing facilities, and on December 8, 1941, the first killing operations began at Chełmno in occupied Poland.

On January 20, 1942, 15 high-ranking Nazi party, SS, and German government officials gathered at a villa in the Berlin suburb of Wannsee to discuss and coordinate the implementation of the "Final Solution." The participants at the conference did not deliberate whether such a plan should be undertaken but instead discussed the mechanics and logistics needed to realize a decision that had already been made. Most of them were already aware that Jews were being killed, but they received a fuller briefing on the scope of the mass-murder program. Nazi planners envisioned that the "Final Solution" would ultimately involve 11 million European Jews from Ireland to the Urals and from Scandinavia to Spain—in short, every Jew in Europe. More than half of the conference participants held doctoral degrees. No one protested the plan or the decision to implement it.

Likewise, the "Final Solution" could not have taken place without the contributions of countless regular citizens who came from all walks of life and all levels of society. Although few thought of themselves as criminals, most understood the consequences of their actions. Some perpetrators had held official office before Hitler's rise to power;

others were newcomers seeking to establish themselves. Some were zealots motivated by Nazi racial ideology; a great many others merely followed orders; still others justified their actions as a defense of their nation, society, and culture against Soviet communism; and, finally, some were motivated by personal gain, jealousy, or revenge.

Most Germans performed small roles in what became a vast undertaking. Using assembly-line techniques, individuals did their jobs within a bureaucratic apparatus that allowed them to remain detached from the consequences of their actions. The participants included high-ranking bureaucrats who helped formulate and implement the "Final Solution" and those who identified and located the victims. They included lawyers who handled the "Aryanization" of property owned by Jews, industrialists who profited from the forced labor of concentration camp inmates, and contractors who built the gas chambers and supplied Zyklon B gas to the SS. In a more direct way, the SS men who operated the killing centers in German-occupied Poland helped, as did the ordinary soldiers and police officials who shot Jews at the edge of mass graves in the Soviet Union. The Nazi leadership depended on the active cooperation of regular people in regular professions, and, at the very least, the silent acquiescence of others who did not carry out Nazi orders directly.

By the summer of 1942, more than 400 ghettos of varying sizes had been established throughout German-occupied eastern Europe. They held more than two million Jews and, in the Warsaw and Łódź ghettos, more than 8,000 Roma. The provisional nature of the ghettos evolved into a semi-permanent one as the Nazis translated the "Final Solution" from concept to reality. The largest of the ghettos included those of Warsaw, Łódź, Sosnowiec, and Białystok in Poland; Minsk in Belorussia; Kovno (present-day Kaunas) and Vilna (present-day Vilnius) in Lithuania; and Riga in Latvia. The larger ghettos were sealed off from the outside world with high walls or fences, along with barbed wire. Signed passes were required to enter or leave, and armed guards stood at entrances and exits.

Smaller ghettos, such as those of Radom, Chelm, and Kielce, were usually surrounded only by a fence, and Jews could enter and leave them with relative ease. Some ghettos, such as Izbica, Piaski, and Bełżyce, encompassed virtually whole towns and were not bordered off at all. Some of the "open" ghettos were short-lived: the SS and police annihilated them after a short period of time, either shooting the inhabitants or deporting them to concentration camps or killing centers. With the Nazi decision for mass murder in 1942, the German authorities began the long and involved process of emptying the ghettos in the occupied east and deporting the inhabitants to killing centers.

As a general rule, the Nazis did not use ghettos in Germany or in western Europe. Beginning in September 1941, the Nazis required all Jews who lived in those areas and were over the age of six to wear the yellow Star of David badge; plus, strict residence ordinances forced the inhabitants into certain areas of the cities, thereby concentrating them in "Jewish buildings." Deportation of Jews from Germany began on October 15, 1941, even before the Germans began construction of the killing centers in occupied Poland. Between October and December 1941, nearly 42,000 Jews were deported from Germany, Austria, and the Czech lands to ghettos in the east and later to the killing centers.

In November 1941, the SS established the Theresienstadt camp-ghetto near the Czech city of Prague in northwest Bohemia. Although it fulfilled the role of both a ghetto and a transit camp by confining Jews until such time as the Germans chose to deport them farther east, Theresienstadt simultaneously served an important propaganda function for the SS. The German authorities repeatedly stated publicly that the deportation of Jews from Germany was part of a resettlement operation, where they would be employed in "productive" labor. The purpose of this deception was primarily for domestic German consumption, because the Nazi leaders feared that public unrest might arise if the population knew exactly what was being done in the killing centers. Hence, the reality of the ghettos, camps, and killing centers could not be publicly confirmed. But how would it look to deport elderly Jews who were clearly unsuitable for labor, and how could one explain the disappearance of prominent Jewish artists, thinkers, writers, and others? The Nazis saw Theresienstadt as a suitable cover to respond to those Germans who were not entirely satisfied with the official explanations of the fate of all German Jews in the east.

In Nazi propaganda, Theresienstadt was presented as a retirement ghetto where German Jews—primarily the elderly; disabled war veterans; or prominently known artists, writers, or entertainers—could live in safety. Eventually, it was portrayed to the International Red Cross and the world at large as a "city" for the Jews, complete with amenities and comforts for adults and children alike. The German public and the International Red Cross, who were permitted access in June 1944, were all too willing to accept this deception, or at least not to probe further. In fact, Theresienstadt served as a transit camp for nearly 70,000 Czech Jews en route to Auschwitz and other ghettos and camps, as well as a temporary residence for nearly 20,000 German and Austrian Jews whom the Germans eventually deported to killing centers. In all, nearly 141,000 German, Austrian, Czech, Danish, Dutch, Slovak, and Hungarian Jews arrived in Theresienstadt during the war. More than 88,000 of them were deported to their deaths, the majority at Auschwitz. Nor was the reality of Theresienstadt itself much different from other ghettos: about 33,500 of its residents died from the harsh conditions in the ghetto.

For the German authorities, the ghettos continued to serve the provisional purpose of concentrating and isolating the Jewish population; but, in reality, the complexity of implementing the "Final Solution" required maintaining many ghettos for years. The

Jews confined there necessarily developed an intricate and involved communal life over time. While daily survival was necessarily dominated by the realities of work, food, shelter, health, and well-being, the Jews in the ghetto—in part through the efforts of the Jewish Councils—also found ways to educate their children, organize cultural and social events, clandestinely observe their faith, and engage in countless other activities that sustained them amid unrelenting deprivation.

GERMAN POLICIES IN WESTERN EUROPE

Almost immediately following the German invasion and the occupation of western Europe in June 1940, the Germans initiated steps that would later facilitate implementing the "Final Solution" there. With varying degrees of help from indigenous governments and officials, they applied the experience gained in Germany to the occupied countries or dependent partners, often initiating an overwhelming barrage of antisemitic laws in rapid succession. For those who were defined as Jews, the Germans, or collaborators, then restricted or eliminated their civil rights, confiscated their property and businesses, and banned them from most professions. Isolated from non-Jews and, in most countries, marked with the yellow Star of David, Jews were without recourse.

The next step for the Nazis was to establish internment or transit camps that would serve as portals from the western European countries to the railways leading to the east. Beginning in 1942, German authorities and their collaborators gathered tens of thousands of Jews in special police transit camps such as Drancy in France, Malines in Belgium, and Westerbork in Holland, where the Jews were confined in limbo for days, weeks, and sometimes months or years. Meanwhile, a steady stream of Jews in transit camps were loaded onto trains and deported to the concentration camps and killing centers in the east.

German anti-Jewish policy in the occupied countries always reflected the goals of the "Final Solution." However, the ultimate fate of each community varied, depending on the degree of control the Germans exercised; the number of Jews; and the level of cooperation the Germans received from indigenous government or other agencies, administrative officials, and individual civilians. In general, foreign and stateless Jews who had taken refuge in western Europe in the 1930s were especially vulnerable. Host countries did not feel obligated to keep or protect those Jews, and indeed, they often viewed them as an unnecessary burden in very trying times. When the Germans demanded Jews for deportation, foreign or stateless Jews were the first to be surrendered.

About 350,000 Jews lived in France at the time of the German invasion. Beginning in March 1942, the French police assisted in carrying out the deportations, both in the German-occupied zone of northern France and in the unoccupied south. By the end of the war, the Germans had deported and killed nearly 75,000 Jews who had resided in France. Meanwhile, in Belgium, the Jewish community numbered about 66,000. From the summer of 1942 to mid 1944, 25,000 Jews—more than one-third—were deported to Auschwitz by way of Belgian transit camps. In the Netherlands, the Dutch civil administration, supervised by the Germans, deported about 107,000 of 140,000 Jews residing in Holland to the killing centers through the transit camps at Westerbork and Amersfoort. Barely more than 5,000 survived.

The transportation of hundreds of thousands of individuals from their homes across the continent of Europe could not have taken place without trains. In that regard, the European rail system played a crucial role in the implementation of the "Final Solution," thereby linking the collection centers, internment and transit camps, and ghettos to labor and concentrations camps and to killing centers where the Jews and others were put to death. The Germans used both freight and passenger cars for the deportations and doubled the number of passengers who could fit in each car to maximize the efficiency of each trip.

Reflecting the high priority of their mission, the transports rolled as often as possible. The Germans did not tell the Jews where they were going, how long the journey would last, or what would happen once they reached their final destination. They also did not provide the deportees with food or water, even when the transports had to wait days on railroad spurs for other trains to pass. The people sealed in freight cars suffered from intense heat in summer and freezing temperatures in winter. Aside from a bucket, no provisions existed for sanitary requirements. Deprived of food and water, many deportees died before the trains reached their destinations. Armed guards accompanying the train transports shot anyone trying to escape.

German transportation officials and local railroad workers could see that large numbers of people arrived at isolated railroad stations in German-occupied Poland and disappeared into makeshift facilities. Local officials, in particular, also saw that the returning trains were either empty or filled with the possessions of those who had just arrived. Most suspected and many knew full well that the SS was killing the Jews who arrived on transport trains at those locations, but no record exists of any railroad employees protesting or resigning. Between the fall of 1941 and the fall of 1944, the German authorities transported millions of people by train to murder sites in occupied Poland and the occupied Soviet Union. After the war, despite the complicity of hundreds of railroad workers, not one German transportation official was convicted of Nazi crimes.

The killing centers fulfilled the singular function of mass murder: the SS and police designed, organized, and operated them to have the capacity so that by the end of the day they could put to death entire transports which had arrived that morning. With the exception of those few selected for work in support of the assembly-line mass murder, no one—not the young, the healthy, or the fit for work—was spared. The first killing center was Chełmno, which began operations in December 1941 on an estate some 30 miles (48.3 kilometers) northwest of Łódź, in German-occupied Poland. On arrival, the SS and police induced or forced the Jews to undress and relinquish their valuables and then herded them into closed paneled trucks. Engineers and mechanics hermetically sealed the trucks and reconfigured the exhaust pipes to pump carbon monoxide exhaust fumes into the back of the truck until those inside were dead. Between December 1941 and July 1944, the SS and police killed 156,000 people at Chełmno, most of them Jews, but about 5,000 were Roma. No victims are known to have escaped.

In 1942 in the General Government, SS and police engineers constructed the killing centers of Bełżec, Sobibór, and Treblinka. The centers functioned in support of Operation Reinhard, one element of which encompassed the murder of all Jews residing in the General Government. Just as Nazi planners had envisioned, the SS and police staffs at those centers could commit mass murder quickly, efficiently, and with minimal oversight; they killed all but a handful of deportees shortly after arrival by means of carbon monoxide gas in stationary gas chambers modeled on the T-4 killing operations.

The camp authorities temporarily spared a small number of "work Jews" to facilitate the process, assisting the deportees off the trains and through the various stages to the gas chambers, all the while being required to calm the victims with reassurances about the future. Others in the labor details removed the corpses and buried them. After the autumn of 1942, when the SS authorities decided to burn the corpses, the forced labor details were required to exhume them and burn them over large outdoor ovens made of rail track. Finally, the killing center authorities deployed Jews to sort through the victims' personal possessions and to prepare them for shipment to Germany. Every few weeks or months, the SS would kill the "work Jews," replacing them with new arrivals. SS and police personnel murdered approximately 1.7 million Jews as part of Operation Reinhard. Very few deportees survived the camps: some 300 survived Sobibór and about 120 survived Treblinka, virtually all as a result of uprisings that occurred in 1943. Only two individuals are known to have survived Bełżec.

The Auschwitz concentration camp, located about 40 miles (64.4 kilometers) west of Kraków in southwestern Poland, was the largest camp complex established by the Germans during World War II. It included a concentration camp–detention facility (Auschwitz I), a killing center (Auschwitz II or Birkenau), and a second concentration camp that served as a hub for a vast string of forced labor camps (Auschwitz III or Monowitz). By spring 1943, Auschwitz-Birkenau had four gas chambers in operation.

Unlike the Operation Reinhard camps, but like other concentration camps that had gas chambers, the Auschwitz-Birkenau camp staff used Zyklon B gas for mass murder. Trains brought Jews almost daily to Auschwitz-Birkenau from Germany itself and virtually every German-occupied country. Prisoners arriving at the camp were sentenced to one of two fates: immediate death or brutal labor under conditions that were frequently lethal. On the basis of selections often casually made when a transport arrived, the SS staff sent the sick, the elderly, pregnant women, and children directly to the gas chambers; healthy-looking male and female prisoners were brought into the camp as forced laborers.

Jewish women, children, and the elderly (left) await deportation at the railroad station in Köszeg, a small town in northwestern Hungary. KÖSZEG, HUNGARY, MAY 1944. USHMM, COURTESY OF MAGYAR NEMZETI MUZEUM TORTENETI FENYKEPTAR

Registered in more or less the same fashion as the inmates of other concentration camps, Auschwitz prisoners had their heads shaved and were issued ragged, striped camp uniforms. They also—unlike other camp inmates—had a number tattooed on the left forearm, a practice initiated at Auschwitz because the camp authorities could not maintain pace in record keeping with the number of deaths and wanted to be certain that the dead could be identified even if the bodies were quickly stripped of their prisoner uniforms. Indeed, tens of thousands perished because of the unbearable living and working conditions. They were packed into bunks in barracks that barely provided shelter, they received little to eat, and they were punished by long hours of physically exhausting labor.

The SS sent almost all children and adolescents under the age of 15 who arrived at Auschwitz immediately to the gas chambers. During the deportation of the Hungarian Jews in 1944, the camp staff on occasion killed as many as 10,000 Jews in a single day. The bodies were incinerated in crematoria adjacent to the gas chambers; in the case of a malfunction, the bodies were burned in open fields. Between the establishment of Auschwitz I in 1940 and the evacuation of the complex in January 1945, the SS at Auschwitz killed about one million Jews and tens of thousands of Roma, Poles, and Soviet prisoners of war.

Lublin concentration camp, which was also known as Majdanek, in German-occupied Poland, was also a site of mass killing. It had served first as a detention center for prisoners of war and was redesignated a concentration camp in February 1943. In all, nearly 100,000 people died in Majdanek. The majority were Jews; other victims included Polish and Soviet civilians, plus Soviet prisoners of war. On November 3, 1943, SS and police units shot 18,000 Jewish prisoners in pits dug behind Majdanek as part of the grotesquely named Operation Harvest Festival. As the victims were led outside the barbed-wire fence of the camp, the Germans broadcast military music to hide the sounds of the shooting. This massacre was the largest single-day shooting operation in the history of the Holocaust.

Gradually, the Jews began to understand the nature and scope of the German killing policy. In response, and despite the overwhelming nature of the assault they faced, Jews organized and carried out armed resistance against their oppressors. They faced tremendous obstacles, including a lack of armaments and training, the hazards of carrying out operations in a hostile zone, the minimal support and even antisemitic hostility from the surrounding population, the necessity of parting with family, and the ever-present Nazi terror. Nevertheless, both as individuals and in organized groups, Jews engaged in opposition efforts in France, Belgium, Belorussia, Lithuania, Poland, and Ukraine. They also fought in national French, Greek, Italian, Soviet, and Yugoslav resistance organizations.

Resistance organizations emerged in more than 100 ghettos in Poland, Lithuania, Belorussia, and Ukraine; and Jews fought back when the Germans attempted to establish ghettos in a number of small towns, including Starodub (now Russia), Kleck (Kletsak), Lachwa, Mir, and Tuczyn (Tuchyn, now Ukraine) in eastern Poland in 1942. As the Germans destroyed major ghettos in 1943, they met with armed Jewish resistance in Kraków, Białystok, Częstochowa, Będzin, Sosnowiec, and Tarnów, as well as a major uprising in Warsaw. Thousands of Jews escaped from the ghettos and joined partisan units in nearby forests. Jews from Minsk, Vilna (present-day Vilnius), Riga, and Kovno (present-day Kaunas) all formed partisan units that engaged in armed resistance. Many ghetto fighters knew that their efforts could not save Jewish masses from destruction, but they fought for the sake of Jewish honor and to avenge the murder of their families, friends, and communities.

The largest and best-known armed resistance effort was the Warsaw ghetto uprising in April–May 1943, which was sparked by rumors that the Nazis would deport the remaining ghetto inhabitants to the Treblinka killing center in German-occupied Poland. As German forces entered the ghetto, members of the Jewish Fighting Organization (*Żydowska Organizacja Bojowa*) pelted German tanks with hand grenades and Molotov cocktails. Hundreds of Jews fought the Germans and their auxiliaries in the streets of the ghetto. Thousands of Jews refused to obey German orders to report to an assembly point for deportation. In the end, the Germans burned the ghetto to the ground to force the Jews out. It took 27 days to destroy the ghetto and crush the last resisters. Although they knew defeat was certain, Jews in the ghetto fought desperately and valiantly.

In western Belorussia, western Ukraine, and eastern Poland, Jewish civilians gathered in camps and assisted Soviet partisan efforts by repairing weapons, making clothing, cooking for the fighters, and participating in active assaults on the Germans. As many as 10,000 Jews survived the war by taking refuge with those partisan units.

Despite the most adverse conditions, Jewish prisoners succeeded in initiating resistance and uprisings in the German camps, as well, and even in the killing centers of Treblinka, Sobibór, and Auschwitz-Birkenau during 1943–44. About 1,000 Jewish prisoners participated in the revolt in Treblinka. On August 2, 1943, Jews seized what weapons they could find— picks, axes, and some firearms stolen from the camp armory—and they set fire to the camp. About 200 managed to escape. The Germans recaptured and killed about half of the escapees. On October 14, 1943, prisoners in Sobibór killed 11 SS guards and police auxiliaries and set the camp on fire. About 300 prisoners escaped, breaking through the barbed wire and risking their lives in the minefield surrounding the camp. More than 100 were recaptured and later shot. On October 7, 1944, prisoners assigned to Crematorium IV at Auschwitz-Birkenau rebelled after learning that they were going to be killed. The Germans crushed the revolt and murdered almost all of the several hundred prisoners involved in the rebellion. Other camp uprisings took place in the Kruszyna (1942), Minsk-Mazowiecki (1943), and Janowska (1943) camps. In several dozen camps, prisoners organized escapes to join partisan units.

In France, the Jewish Army (*Armée Juive*), a French Jewish partisan group, was founded in Toulouse in January 1942. Composed of members of Zionist youth movements, the Jewish Army operated in and around Toulouse, as well as Lyon, Nice, and Paris. Its members smuggled money from Switzerland into France to assist Jews in hiding; smuggled at least 500 Jews and non-Jews into neutral Spain; and took part in the 1944 uprisings against the Germans in Lyon, Paris, and Toulouse.

The Union of Jews for Resistance and Mutual Aid (more commonly known as *Solidarité*) was a Jewish Communist organization that carried out attacks on German personnel in Paris. Many Jews joined the general French resistance as well. In Belgium, a combined Jewish and non-Jewish resistance unit (also named *Solidarité*) derailed a deportation train in April 1943. On July 25, 1942, Jewish resisters attacked and burned the files of the Association of Jews in Belgium, which had functioned—at German direction—as a Jewish Council. Jews were also active in the Dutch and Italian underground movements.

The effect of armed Jewish resistance should not be exaggerated. In part because of existing antisemitism among the surrounding populations, Jewish partisans received little help. Their isolation was reinforced by the fact that the Allies failed to provide arms and explosives, and their effectiveness was severely hindered by the all-encompassing strength and power of the enemy. In the end, Jewish resistance efforts did little to stop the Germans from mass-murdering the Jews.

In addition to participating in armed operations, Jews resisted the Nazis by focusing on aid to those in hiding, rescue, escape, and spiritual defiance. Jews in the ghettos and camps also responded to Nazi oppression by creating and sustaining cultural institutions, continuing religious observance, and undertaking efforts to document their experiences under Nazi oppression. Individuals and groups attempted to preserve their history, culture, communal life, and evidence of their destruction through diaries, testimonies, communal records, poetry, song, and art. Their efforts can be seen as a counterpart to armed resistance: not by killing the enemy, but by attempting to preserve the dignity of the victims and to leave behind a record of their existence in the world.

As the tide of the war shifted and it became clear that the Allies were gaining ground, the SS was faced with the problem of concealing the evidence of mass killing. It was a daunting prospect because the camps had to be dismantled and untold numbers of dead had to be exhumed and cremated. The SS tried to conceal their traces both by burning bodies and by destroying documentation that testified to their crimes.

The Operation Reinhard killing centers were dismantled in 1943: Bełżec, which had ceased operations in December 1942, was dismantled in the spring; Treblinka, where the prisoner revolt in August 1943 effectively halted operations, was closed in the autumn; and Sobibór, where operations as a killing center ended with the prisoner revolt, was closed at the end of the year. After their work was finished, the SS and police murdered the prisoners who had been forced to dismantle the camps. The sites where Bełżec and Treblinka had been located were plowed over, relandscaped, and camouflaged as small farms. After the gassing facilities had been removed at Sobibór, the camp served for a time as an ammunition depot for the *Waffen* SS. The SS continued to murder those arriving at

Auschwitz-Birkenau until November 1944, when, at Himmler's order, the SS destroyed the killing apparatus as Soviet forces approached the area.

After the catastrophic German defeats at Stalingrad in January 1943 and in Kursk in July 1943 on the eastern front, Security Police and Security Service officials in the occupied Soviet Union also took steps to conceal the traces of the shooting operations carried out in 1941–42. Throughout the occupied Soviet Union, SS and police forces identified mass graves and then deployed forced labor detachments of Jews to exhume the partially decomposed bodies and burn them on open-air pyres built on rail tracks. After the job was complete, the SS and police killed the Jews whom they had forced to carry out the gruesome tasks.

In January 1945, Nazi Germany faced total military defeat. As Allied and Soviet forces approached the camps, the SS organized the remaining prisoners into columns and marched them away from the advancing armies. Those evacuations came to be called "death marches" as prisoners—Jewish and non-Jewish—were made to traverse hundreds of miles in bitter cold, with little or no food, water, or rest. Any prisoner unable to keep up with the others was shot. The largest death marches took place in the winter of 1944–45 as the Soviet army liberated Poland.

The SS camp guards reacted in different ways to total defeat. Some took off their uniforms and tried to disappear among the millions of German army POWs. Others, remaining faithful to Nazi ideology, viewed the Allied victory as the handiwork of the Jews and thus attempted to fulfill their mission by killing as many Jews as possible in the final moments of the war. Still others carried out massacres to prevent Jewish survivors from falling into the hands of the liberators and publicly testifying to the Nazi atrocities.

As Germany fell into complete collapse, the converging armies of the Allies and the Soviets arrived in the concentration camps. The typical brutality and lethal nature of camp life was exacerbated in those last months by the total breakdown of supplies, often limiting or eliminating what little food the prisoners were getting. Liberators confronted piles of unburied corpses and barracks filled with dead and dying prisoners. The stench of death was everywhere. Even though the structures of assembly-line mass murder had been destroyed, liberation exposed the full scope of Nazi horrors to the world. Despite Nazi efforts to hide their traces, thousands of starved and diseased prisoners had been left behind to testify—both in words and by their physical condition—about their experiences in the camps.

Even after liberation, thousands of prisoners continued to die at a high rate. The lack of sanitary conditions in the camps intensified the problem, contributing to outbreaks of epidemics. Within a few days, half the prisoners found alive when the Soviets arrived at Auschwitz had died. In Bergen-Belsen, hundreds of prisoners died every day for three weeks. During the first month after liberation, 13,000 of the camp's approximately 50,000 surviving prisoners died. Even at the sites of the killing centers, which the SS and police had dismantled, forensic evidence, such as buried ash and bone fragments, bore witness to the crimes committed there.

World War II ended in Europe with the unconditional surrender of the German armed forces to the Western Allies on May 7, 1945, and to the Soviets on May 9, 1945. May 8, 1945, was proclaimed Victory in Europe Day (V-E Day). One week earlier, as Soviet forces neared his command bunker in central Berlin on April 30, 1945, Adolf Hitler committed suicide. It is no exaggeration to say that Europe lay in ruins. War and genocide, displacement and upheaval left the continent in a state of chaos. Although trials of the perpetrators began within months of the German surrender, western European Jewish communities would take decades to partially restore themselves. The Jewish communities of central and eastern Europe disappeared, culturally and physically, except for remnants in Hungary and Romania and small groups of survivors elsewhere in the region. Indeed, what was destroyed during the 12 years of Nazi rule—human life, culture, history, community, and collective memory—could be never be rebuilt or repaired.

Shortly following the liberation in April 1945, emaciated survivors (right) rest in a group at the Buchenwald concentration camp in Germany. BUCHENWALD, GERMANY, C. APRIL 11, 1945. USHMM, COURTESY OF HADASSAH BIMKO ROSENSAFT

According to Nazi ideology, the Jews of Europe represented the priority "racial" enemy who by their very existence threatened the survival of the "Aryan" German race. Drawing

Despite Nazi efforts to hide their traces

thousands of starved and diseased prisonors

had been left behind to testify

—both in words and by their physical condition—

about their experiences in the camps

on a thousand years of stereotypes about Jews and "Jewish" behavior, as well as recent malicious stereotyping linking Jews to Bolshevik radicalism, the Nazis enlisted a nation of more than 60 million and hundreds of thousands of collaborators from annexed, occupied, and allied countries in a program to physically annihilate the Jewish population of Europe. In terms of numbers alone, they almost succeeded; the Germans and their Axis partners killed up to six million European Jews living in the territory that they had seized.

Perhaps 1.5 million Jews survived this unprecedented, murderous onslaught, the vast majority of whom either lived on the land controlled by Germany's Axis partners or managed to flee German-occupied Europe. Many of those who survived the camps, killing centers, and shooting operations would have to recover from having witnessed the physical elimination of their families and communities. Moreover, by virtually eliminating the Jewish minority in central and eastern Europe, the Nazi program of mass murder tore asunder forever an integral part of Central and East European society and culture, in both the cities and the countryside. Although individual, national cultures could revive, even after 40 years of Communist rule, they lack—to this day—that unique flavor, diversity, and complexity that their Jewish communities contributed over the course of a millennium to their development. As for the survivors of the Nazi assault, they brought their creativity, talents, hopes, and hard work to the lands and peoples that offered them refuge and a chance to start anew during and after the era of the Holocaust.

EPILOGUE | THE AFTERMATH OF THE HOLOCAUST:

Punishing and Preventing the Crime of Genocide

THE HOLOCAUST AND OTHER NAZI CRIMES WERE NEITHER THE INEVITABLE OUTCOME of a process set in motion by Adolf Hitler in 1933, nor the preordained result of the development of his and other Nazi party leaders' beliefs. To the contrary, the citizens who participated in or simply stood by and watched Nazi atrocities faced daily choices. The momentum of their actions as individuals over time propelled European society into unprecedented violence and systematized mass murder.

In the wake of Nazi Germany's defeat, the Allies faced a challenge: What should they do with a German nation that had made the Holocaust possible? What actions could be taken to bring culpable individuals to account and to return public life to an acceptable course? In addition to restoring order and physically rebuilding, the Allied leadership sought ways to confront the lingering effects of Nazi ideology. This effort, called "denazi-fication," aimed at uprooting and eradicating all traces of Nazism in German society. This activity included confiscating and destroying books; monitoring radio stations, magazines, movies, and other public media; and destroying symbols, such as the swastika, that could contribute to the persistence of Nazi ideals and beliefs.

Among the most important efforts to reeducate and recivilize Germany was the criminal prosecution of Nazi perpetrators for crimes committed by the Nazi leadership and innumerable ordinary citizens. In 1945, the victorious Allied powers (the United States, the United Kingdom, France, and Soviet Russia) established the International Military Tribunal at Nuremberg for that purpose. After legal experts had labored over new concepts in international law to facilitate proceedings involving such unprecedented crimes, the tribunal indicted 22 senior officials of the Nazi regime on four charges: war crimes, crimes against peace, crimes against humanity, and conspiracy to commit each of those crimes. In the course of the trial, the tribunal rejected the long-standing doctrine of sovereign immunity, which exempted heads of state from prosecution for actions taken while in office, and the doctrine of superior orders, which protected subordinates from being prosecuted for crimes they committed as a result of a direct order. As U.S. Chief Prosecutor Justice Robert Jackson explained, "[T]he combination of these two doctrines means that nobody is responsible. Society as modernly organized cannot tolerate so broad an area of official irresponsibility."

Chief U.S. prosecutor Justice Robert Jackson (left) delivers the prosecution's opening statement against leading German officials at the International Military Tribunal war crimes trial at Nuremberg in November 1945. NUREMBERG, GERMANY, NOVEMBER 21, 1945. USHMM, COURTESY OF HARRY S. TRUMAN LIBRARY

The Nuremberg Trial brought major Nazi war criminals publicly to justice, exposing evidence of their guilt to the world. Of 21 defendants, 18 were convicted (one defendant committed suicide upon receiving the indictment); 12 were sentenced to death. As important as the convictions were the acquittals, which gave the Nuremberg Trial immediate and long-standing credibility. Each Nuremberg defendant had been granted a genuine opportunity to defend himself in the courtroom. In three cases, the evidence was insufficient to convict the defendants of legal responsibility, and they were acquitted. Signaling an intention to prosecute lesser perpetrators, the tribunal also found three organizations—the SS, the Gestapo and Security Service, and the Nazi Party Leadership Corps—to be criminal entities in which membership potentially constituted a crime.

Following the initial trial, the International Military Tribunal (staffed exclusively with U.S. prosecutors and judges), held 12 subsequent trials at Nuremberg for second-rank Nazi offenders. Those trials focused on members of the military, political, and economic leadership of Germany during the Third Reich, and included as defendants the doctors, judges, policemen, captains of industry, ministry officials, soldiers, and others who had helped realize the ideological goals of the Nazi regime, sometimes personally profiting from their service.

Finally, each victorious Allied power conducted dozens of trials in its allotted zone of occupation in Germany, with lower-level Nazis and non-Nazi perpetrators as defendants. In the U.S. zone alone, nearly 1,700 defendants were tried in 462 separate proceedings. By prosecuting and convicting low-ranking officials, Allied judges maintained the principle of individual legal responsibility for criminal acts while at the same time conveying in no uncertain terms that the acceptance, participation, and cooperation of people at every level of German society had facilitated Nazi crimes.

Among those working with the U.S. prosecution team to prepare for the Nuremberg trials was Raphael Lemkin, a Polish Jewish jurist who had escaped Nazi persecution and emigrated to the United States, but who had lost 49 members of his family, including his parents, during the Holocaust. Dedicating himself to ending such violence in the world, he was the first to give a name to the mass murder that had taken place, coining the term genocide" in his 1944 work *Axis Rule in Occupied Europe*. "By 'genocide' we mean the "destruction of a nation or of an ethnic group," Lemkin wrote. "It is intended ... to signify a coordinated plan of different actions aiming at the destruction of essential foundations of the life of national groups, with the aim of annihilating the groups themselves." Lemkin was able to get the word "genocide" included in the indictment against Nazi leadership, but the tribunal failed to define it as a specific crime in international law.

Lemkin was determined to see the concept of genocide incorporated into international law. He began lobbying at early sessions of the United Nations and worked to enlist the support of national delegations and influential leaders. His efforts eventually resulted in the United Nations' approval of the Convention on the Prevention and Punishment of Genocide on December 9, 1948. The convention established genocide as an international crime that signatory nations "undertake to prevent and punish." As defined in terms of the convention, *genocide* means the intent to destroy, in whole or in part, a national, ethnic, racial, or religious group by killing members of the group; causing serious bodily or mental harm to members of the group; deliberately inflicting on the group conditions of life calculated to bring about its physical destruction in whole or in part; imposing measures intended to prevent births within the group; and/or forcibly transferring children of the group to another group.

The Nuremberg trials and the 1948 Genocide Convention are two of the lasting legacies of the postwar period. From a legal standpoint, the Nuremberg trials provided a precedent for holding individuals at all levels of society accountable for criminal acts on behalf of their government or society. The existence of this precedent inspired the postwar development of an international criminal court to conduct criminal proceedings against individuals accused of genocide, mass murder, torture, and other crimes. From a diplomatic perspective, the Genocide Convention created a framework in which nations could hold one another responsible for the protection of human rights and a legal definition to develop indictments. Both were groundbreaking efforts to establish standards of international conduct that are not subject to changing political, social, or religious forces. But even with those legal and diplomatic mechanisms in place, the postwar period has witnessed ethnic cleansing in Bosnia, genocide in Rwanda, and resurgent antisemitism in many parts of the world, including lands in which the Holocaust took place.

In spite of calls of "never again," beginning in 2003 an ongoing genocide in Darfur, Sudan, gave daily evidence of a militia committing mass murder and rape, killing children, burning villages, and imposing wanton violence based on ethnic, racial, and tribal hatred. Those events test the limits of our faith in legal and diplomatic approaches to the problem of mass genocide. As society has so vividly become aware, a definition of genocide and even a collective commitment to hold those who commit it accountable are not enough to prevent it. Our inability to prevent genocide, however, does not absolve us of our responsibility to bring its perpetrators to justice. At the time of this writing, the International Criminal Court in The Hague indicts, prosecutes, and, if the evidence is sufficient, convicts perpetrators of the genocidal acts in Bosnia and Rwanda.

In this context, it is worth remembering that even during the Holocaust, some individuals saw through what psychologist Eva Fogelman has called "the gauze of Nazi euphemisms." Despite the indifference of most and the collaboration of others, those individuals—from all religious backgrounds and every European country—risked their lives to help Jews and other victims of the Nazi regime. In the end, the actions of individuals to protect human lives, human rights, and human dignity are the ultimate bulwark against abuses of human rights and genocide. As General Roméo Dallaire, head of a small peace-keeping force in Rwanda in 1993 who helplessly watched as the United Nations failed to stop the genocide of 800,000 Tutsis by Hutus, has said, "You've got to start wondering about the depth of your belief in the moral values, the ethical values, and your belief in humanity. All humans are human. There are no humans more human than others. That's it."

FURTHER READING AND ADDITIONAL SOURCES

NAZI IDEOLOGY

Berenbaum, Michael. *A Mosaic of Victims: Non-Jews Persecuted and Murdered by the Nazis.* New York: New York University Press, 1990.

Burleigh, Michael, and Wolfang Wippermann. *The Racial State: Germany, 1933–1945.* New York: Cambridge University Press, 1991.

Cameron, Norman, R. H. Stevens, and Hugh Redwald Trevor-Roper, eds. *Hitler's Table Talk, 1941–44: His Secret Conversations.* New York: Enigma Books, 2000.

Jäckel, Eberhard. *Hitler's World View: A Blueprint for Power.* Cambridge, Mass.: Harvard University Press, 1981.

Mosse, George L. *Toward the Final Solution: A History of European Racism.* Madison: University of Wisconsin Press, 1985.

POLITICAL OPPONENTS, JEHOVAH'S WITNESSES, AND HOMOSEXUALS

Giles, Geoffrey J. *Why Bother about Homosexuals?: Homophobia and Sexual Politics in Nazi Germany.* Washington, D.C.: United States Holocaust Memorial Museum, 2001.

Graffard, Sylvie, and Michel Reynaud. *The Jehovah's Witnesses and the Nazis: Persecution, Deportation, and Murder, 1933–1945.* New York: Cooper Square Press, 2001.

Grau, Günter. *Hidden Holocaust?: Gay and Lesbian Persecution in Germany, 1933–45.* Chicago: Fitzroy Dearborn, 1995.

Hesse, Hans, ed. *Persecution and Resistance of Jehovah's Witnesses during the Nazi Regime, 1933–1945.* Bremen, Germany: Edition Temmen, 2001.

King, Christine Elizabeth. *The Nazi State and the New Religions: Five Case Studies in Non-Conformity.* New York: Edwin Mellen Press, 1982.

Lautmann, Rudiger, Erhard Vismar, and Jack Nusan Porter. *Sexual Politics in the Third Reich: The Persecution of the Homosexuals during the Holocaust.* Newton Highlands, Mass.: The Spencer Press, 1997.

Mommsen, Hans. *Alternatives to Hitler: German Resistance under the Third Reich.* Princeton, N.J.: Princeton University Press, 2003.

Plant, Richard. *The Pink Triangle: The Nazi War against Homosexuals.* New York: H. Holt, 1986.

Schoenberner, Gerhard. *Artists against Hitler: Persecution, Exile, Resistance.* Bonn: Inter Nationes, 1984.

Tarrant, V. E. *The Red Orchestra.* New York: John Wiley & Sons, 1996.

POLISH AND SOVIET CIVILIANS, AND SOVIET PRISONERS OF WAR

Glantz, David M. *When Titans Clashed: How the Red Army Stopped Hitler.* Lawrence: University
Press of Kansas, 1995.

Hirschfeld, Gerhard. *The Policies of Genocide: Jews and Soviet Prisoners of War in Nazi Germany.*
Boston: Allan & Unwin, 1986.

Lukas, Richard. *The Forgotten Holocaust: The Poles under German Occupation, 1939–1944.*
New York: Hippocrene, 1997.

Lukas, Richard. *Out of the Inferno: Poles Remember the Holocaust.* Lexington: University
Press of Kentucky, 1989.

Rowinski, Leokadia. *That the Nightingale Return: Memoir of the Polish Resistance, the Warsaw
Uprising and German P.O.W. Camps.* Jefferson, N.C.: McFarland, 1999.

GERMANS WITH MENTAL AND PHYSICAL DISABILITIES, AFRICAN GERMANS, AND ROMA

Benedict, Susan. "Caring While Killing: Nursing in the 'Euthanasia' Centers." In *Experience
and Expression: Women, the Nazis, and the Holocaust,* eds. Elizabeth R. Baer and Myrna
Goldenberg, pp. 95–110. Detroit: Wayne State University Press, 2003.

Biesold, Horst. *Crying Hands: Eugenics and Deaf People in Nazi Germany.* Washington, D.C.:
Gallaudet University Press, 1999.

Burleigh, Michael. *Death and Deliverance: "Euthanasia" in Germany c. 1900–1945.* New York:
Cambridge University Press, 1994.

Campt, Tina. *Other Germans: Black Germans and the Politics of Race, Gender, and Memory in the
Third Reich.* Ann Arbor: University of Michigan, 2004.

Duna, William A., and Paul Polansky. *The Hidden Holocaust of the Gypsies.* Minneapolis:
Sa-Roma, 1997.

Fings, Karola, Herbert Heuss, and Frank Sparing. *From "Race Science" to the Camps: The Gypsies
during the Second World War.* Hertfordshire, United Kingdom: University of Hertfordshire
Press, 1997.

Friedlander, Henry. *The Origins of Nazi Genocide: From Euthanasia to the Final Solution.* Chapel
Hill: University of North Carolina Press, 1995.

Friedman, Philip. "The Extermination of the Gypsies." In *Genocide and Human Rights: A Global
Anthology,* ed. Jack Nusan Porter, pp. 151–57. Washington, D.C.: University Press of America, 1982.

Hancock, Ian. *Land of Pain: Five Centuries of Gypsy Slavery and Persecution.* Buda, Tex.: World
Romani Union, 1986.

Kenrick, Donald, and Grattan Puxon. *Gypsies under the Swastika.* Hertfordshire, United Kingdom:
Gypsy Research Centre, University of Hertfordshire Press, 1995.

Kesting, Robert W. "Forgotten Victims: Blacks in the Holocaust." *Journal of Negro History* 77, no. 1 (1992): 30–36.

Lewy, Guenther. *The Nazi Persecution of the Gypsies.* Oxford: Oxford University Press, 2000.

Lifton, Robert Jay. *The Nazi Doctors: Medical Killing and the Psychology of Genocide.* New York: Basic Books, 1986.

Lusane, Clarence. *Hitler's Black Victims: The Historical Experiences of Afro-Germans, European Blacks, Africans, and African Americans in the Nazi Era.* New York: Routledge, 2002.

Massaquoi, Hans J. *Destined to Witness: Growing Up Black in Nazi Germany.* New York: William Morrow, 1999.

Proctor, Robert. *Racial Hygiene: Medicine under the Nazis.* Cambridge, Mass.: Harvard University Press, 1988.

Tebbutt, Susan, ed. *Sinti and Roma: Gypsies in German-Speaking Society and Literature.* New York: Berghahn Books, 1998.

United States Holocaust Memorial Museum. *Deadly Medicine: Creating the Master Race.* Washington, D.C.: United States Holocaust Memorial Museum, 2004.

THE DESTRUCTION OF EUROPEAN JEWRY

Arad, Yitzhak, et al. *The Einsatzgruppen Reports: Selections from the Dispatches of the Nazi Death Squads' Campaign Against the Jews, July 1941–January 1943.* New York: Holocaust Library, 1989.

Bauer, Yehuda. *A History of the Holocaust.* New York: Franklin Watts, 2001.

Berenbaum, Michael, et al., eds. *The Holocaust and History: The Known, the Unknown, the Disputed, and the Reexamined.* Bloomington: Indiana University Press, 1998.

Bergen, Doris L. *War & Genocide: A Concise History of the Holocaust.* Lanham, Md.: Rowman & Littlefield, 2003.

Breitman, Richard. *The Architect of Genocide: Himmler and the Final Solution.* New York: Knopf; distributed by Random House, 1991.

Breitman, Richard, and Allen Kraut. *American Refugee Policy and European Jewry, 1933–1945.* Bloomington: Indiana University Press, 1987.

Encyclopedia of the Holocaust. New York: MacMillan, 1990.

Gilbert, Martin. *Auschwitz and the Allies.* New York: Holt, Rinehart, and Winston, 1981.

Hilberg, Raul. *The Destruction of the European Jews.* New Haven, Conn.: Yale University Press, 2003.

Kogon, Eugen, Hermann Langbein, and Adalbert Rückerl, eds. *Nazi Mass Murder: A Documentary History of the Use of Poison Gas.* New Haven, Conn.: Yale University Press, 1993.

Kurek, Ewa. *Your Life Is Worth Mine: How Polish Nuns Saved Hundreds of Jewish Children in German-Occupied Poland, 1939–1945.* New York: Hippocrene Books, 1997.

Morse, Arthur. *While Six Million Died: A Chronicle of American Apathy.* Woodstock, N.Y.: Overlook Press, 1998.

Sloyan, Gerald, ed. *Ethics in the Shadow of the Holocaust: Christian and Jewish Perspectives.* Franklin, Wis.: Sheed & Ward, 2001.

THE AFTERMATH OF THE HOLOCAUST

Eltringham, Nigel. *Accounting for Horror: Post-Genocide Debates in Rwanda.* London and Sterling, Va.: Pluto Press, 2004.

Marrus, Michael R. *The Nuremberg War Crimes Trial, 1945–46: A Documentary History.* Boston: Bedford Books, 1997.

Power, Samantha. *"A Problem from Hell": America and the Age of Genocide.* New York: Basic Books, 2002.

Smith, Helmut Walser, ed. *The Holocaust and Other Genocides: History, Representation, Ethics.* Nashville, Tenn.: Vanderbilt University Press, 2002.

Tent, James F. *Mission on the Rhine: Reeducation and Denazification in American-Occupied Germany.* Chicago: University of Chicago Press, 1982.

Totten, Samuel, William S. Parsons, Israel W. Charny, eds. *A Century of Genocide: Critical Essays and Eyewitness Accounts.* New York: Routledge, 2004.

INDEX

DESIGN
Studio A, Alexandria, Va.
www.studioa.com

PRINTING
Mount Vernon Printing

TYPE
Scala
ScalaSans

PAPER
Mohawk Options